INTRODUCTION

It has become increasingly common to observe that the global balance of power is shifting from West to East. Commentators have recently argued that the twenty-first century will be an "Asian century,"[1] that the "political and economic axis of the world . . . is shifting east"[2] and that we are now entering a "Eurasian era."[3] Others see Asia's rise as leading to a more balanced, "multipolar" world,[4] since there are a number of increasingly prominent multilateral institutions bringing together Asian powers, which are acting as counterbalances to their Western equivalents.

The last few centuries have seen a Eurocentric world emerge, with the U.S. coming to dominate during the twentieth century. European colonialism brought about an unprecedented fragmentation of the Asian landmass. For many hundreds of years prior to this, Asia was a highly connected continent with extensive trade networks and continual movement of people and ideas. The Mongol empire in the thirteenth and fourteenth centuries united the entirety of the Silk Road, a huge network of trade routes stretching across Eurasia from China to Europe, under one political system. During this time, Europe was largely cut off from this prosperous Asian trade network.[5] A powerful and interconnected Asian continent is not something new, therefore, but a phenomenon that once existed for many centuries.

The gradual undoing of colonial power relations in recent years has allowed Asian countries to form deeper and different connections with their immediate neighbours. China's Belt and Road Initiative, as the most ambitious economic initiative of our times, is widely understood to be the greatest exemplification of this power shift from West to East.

In 2013, whilst visiting Kazakhstan's capital city, Chinese president Xi Jinping announced his plan to establish a land-based "Economic Belt along the Silk Road" aiming to connect China to Europe. Shortly after this, Xi visited Indonesia and proposed to build "the 21st century Maritime Silk Road" with the Association of Southeast Asian Nations (ASEAN), which would link China both to the Mediterranean and to the South Pacific. These two initiatives were initially seen as being separate, the first dealing with Asian-European and the second with China-ASEAN relationships. However, by the time that China promulgated its "Visions and Actions on Jointly Building the Silk Road Economic Belt and 21st Century Maritime Silk Road" in March 2015, the two initiatives had together come to be termed the Belt and Road Initiative (BRI), perceived as the cornerstone of China's foreign policy.

According to the Chinese narrative, the BRI aims to revive the ancient land-based and maritime Silk Roads by connecting East Asia with Europe. To achieve its goal, China plans to improve connectivity in specific areas between the East Asian and European economic networks and link these areas up to cover the whole Eurasian region. By doing so, it hopes to "promote the free flow of economic factors (like capital, labour, and goods), highly efficient allocation of resources and deep integration of markets across the region."[6] The improved connectivity is expected to result in greater economic cooperation and create opportunities for economic development, both for China itself and for the other countries along the Belt and Road. The goal of improving connectivity includes cooperation in five areas: coordinating development policies; forging infrastructure and facilities networks; strengthening investment and trade relations; enhancing financial cooperation; and deepening social and cultural exchanges. The BRI is a long-term plan: the project has been estimated to take roughly thirty-five years to complete.[7] The geographical scope of the BRI is huge. The Belt, on land, aims to connect East Asia to Central Asia, West Asia, and Europe. The Maritime Silk Road is described as consisting of two sea routes, one connecting China's coast to Europe through the South China Sea and the Indian Ocean, and the other from China's coast through the South China Sea to the South Pacific. Six "corridors" of economic cooperation are envisaged, spanning Asia, Europe and Africa, based on international transport routes, core cities and key ports. These economic corridors will be the New Eurasia Land Bridge, China-Mongolia-Russia, China-Central Asia-West Asia, China-Indochina Peninsula, China-Pakistan, and Bangladesh-China-India-Myanmar (Fig. I.1). According to this plan, the BRI will cover at least sixty-five countries and around two thirds of the world's population.

The notion of "corridors" is, however, somewhat misleading. Chinese scholar Dr Ma Bin has pointed out that whilst numerous maps of the BRI have been produced, there is no official map: these unofficial maps of the BRI have led to a misunderstanding of the initiative as consisting of uninterrupted trade and transport routes, whereas the BRI also puts a lot of emphasis on Foreign Direct Investment, which is not necessarily about geographical connectivity.[8] It is also the case that on the ground, the BRI consists of a series of distinct projects, and that there are still substantial barriers to the connectivity China hopes to achieve.

This is one important difference between the BRI and the "Silk Road," which is invoked because the BRI centres around pan-Eurasian trade, with the six land-based "corridors" being loosely based on the ancient network of routes used by traders crossing Eurasia. Another key difference between the BRI and the ancient Silk Road is the centrality of energy projects to the BRI: the majority of these are coal, oil and gas projects, though renewable energy projects are growing in number.[9]

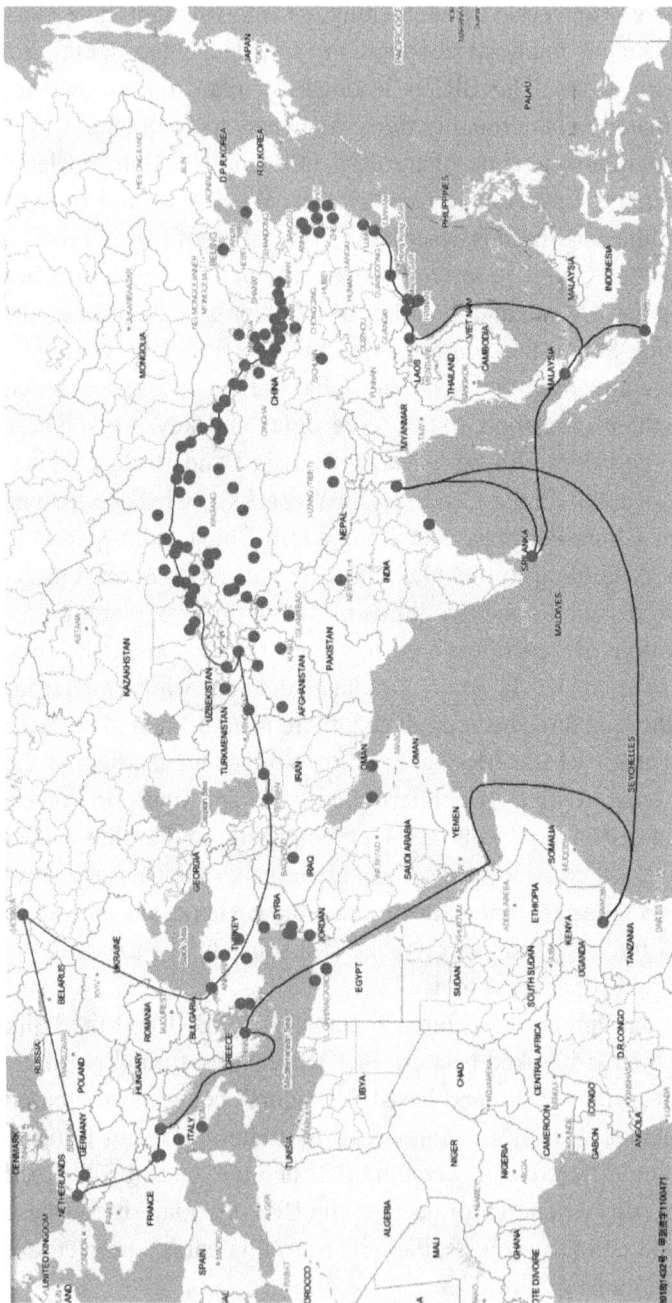

Figure I.1. The 21st Century Maritime Silk Road and the six overland corridors of the Silk Road Economic Belt. Source: World Bank. (2019). Belt and Road Economics: Opportunities and Risks of Transport Corridors. Washington, DC: World Bank. License: Creative Commons Attribution CC BY 3.0 IGO.

CHINA'S MOTIVATIONS

Such an ambitious initiative has aroused heated international debate around Beijing's motivation and the mechanisms through which it will implement the BRI agenda. With regards to motives, the BRI is widely regarded by outside commentators as Beijing's mega foreign policy, designed to achieve its geopolitical purposes. Beijing, conversely, insists that the BRI is about economic development and win-win cooperation rather than geopolitical strategy. However, there has been much speculation about China's unstated or hidden intentions, amounting to a somewhat "paranoid" interpretation of the project.[10] This is unsurprising given that suspicion of China has a long history in European analyses of international relations.

The potential motivations presented in this section are based on arguments put forward by scholars and commentators, and are not fully substantiated by statements from Beijing itself. Onlookers perceive that from China's perspective, the BRI could resolve a number of economic and other issues for both China and its neighbours. One pressing economic issue in China at present is its overcapacity in steel production. Firms producing construction materials, which have become accustomed to massive government spending on domestic infrastructure projects, now risk sitting idle, without sufficiently large markets to absorb their production. BRI infrastructure projects including roads, railways and ports in BRI states could boost demand for raw materials, which will help China to alleviate its overcapacity, and also enable Chinese companies to gain a footprint in international markets.[11] BHP, one of the world's largest producers of iron ore (an ingredient in steel-making) identified four hundred core projects worth $1.3tn under the BRI and predicted that this could increase steel demand by an additional 15m tonnes and double the growth rate of steel demand in China over the next decade.[12] The BRI may also benefit Chinese firms by motivating them to rethink their strategies, for example by moving production out of China to take advantage of lower labour costs elsewhere and using the newly built infrastructure to facilitate exports to China and international markets.[13]

The improved transport infrastructure could also reduce the transport cost for Chinese imports. For example, China has traditionally imported most of its oil and commodities through the South China Sea. But importing goods from the Middle East overland through the Gwadar Port in Pakistan reduces the distance travelled by ninety percent.[14] These factors taken together are expected to help China to mitigate the economic slowdown it has experienced in recent years, especially since its trade war with the US.

A further motivation for economic development stems from the fact that the western parts of China have suffered economically in the last four decades. These are landlocked areas which have been left behind in terms of economic development in comparison to the eastern regions, which are closer to the coast and have therefore benefited from China's maritime export strategy. Their lack of development also results from an incapacity to drive substantial economic growth from cooperation with neighbours to the west, such as Central Asia and India.[15] In 2013, per capita income in western provinces such as Gansu, Guizhou, Qinghai and Xinjiang was only between a third and a half of that in eastern provinces such as Guangdong, Fujian and Zhejiang.[16] In 2000, Beijing launched the Great West Development Program, which intended to open up the western part of the country. However, by 2015 it was estimated that the region was still going to need thirty to fifty years to "catch up" with the rest of China.[17] In the design of the Belt and Road Initiative, this western region is designated as the core area of the land-based Silk Road Economic Belt (SREB). More specifically, the region serves as the hub for three out of the six proposed economic corridors, namely, the New Eurasian Land Bridge, the China-Central Asia-West Asia corridor, and the China-Pakistan corridor. Beijing's plan is that the improved economic and infrastructural connectivity with the states in South Asia and Central Asia—which themselves will be undergoing economic development due to BRI projects—will speed up the development of the western provinces of China and therefore address the country's regional development disparity.[18]

China has prevalent economic interests in, and few conflicts with, the states in the heartland of Eurasia (excepting India, with which it has strained relations). China thus has more space there to act as a regional power to improve its position in the international community and construct international norms and institutions for long-term interests—as Callahan argues, the BRI is part of a new Chinese "peripheral diplomacy" (*zhou bian wai jiao*), presented as a shift of the focus of Beijing's diplomacy from its relationship with the US to Asia.[19]

Beijing may also hope that the BRI will improve China's security as a nation. Through the BRI, China aims to establish improved energy and transport infrastructure connections to energy suppliers from the Middle East and Central Asia: this diversification of its energy supply will reduce the country's current vulnerability. Furthermore, by including historically turbulent countries in Central Asia and South Asia (such as Afghanistan and Pakistan) as participants in the Initiative, China hopes to reduce political unrest and conflict in these regions by promoting connectivity and boosting trade and investment.[20] This would bring China a peaceful peripheral security environment. China also has domestic security concerns: the Xinjiang Uyghur Autonomous Region in the West of China is an area which has long been rife with economic discontent and political tension, which has culminated in outbreaks of violence. China hopes to ameliorate the political tension in this region by stimulating cross-border trade with the neighbouring Central Asian countries and thus bringing greater prosperity to Xinjiang.[21]

The BRI could also serve to promote China's financial power in the international arena, where for decades the dollar has served as the global reserve currency. China has long been disappointed by the malfunctioning of the existing dollar-centric global financial institutions (such as the IMF and World Bank) as well as the slow progress made in reforming them. Established to serve primarily the interests of the US and adopting the US' neoliberal economic approach, they have proven unable to accommodate the rapid rise of East Asian economies, including China. Credit offered by Chinese institutions for projects falling under the framework of the BRI may increase the volume of Bilateral Swap Agreements (BSA) between the People's Bank of China and countries wanting to swap their currencies for the Renminbi (RMB).[22] Some have argued that this trend will bring in a dramatic shift away from the dollar-based financial system to an RMB-based one.[23] Others, however, believe that there is still a long way to go for the RMB to replace U.S. dollars as the global reserve currency. Nonetheless, the establishment of the New Development Bank and the Asian Infrastructure Investment Bank (AIIB) have enabled China's financial ties to neighbouring countries to become "more formal and far-reaching," and this is giving "greater focus and strategic leverage to China's capital exports."[24] Another potentially transformative recent development in this area has been the decision made by the 8 member states of the Shanghai Cooperation Organisation (China, Russia, Kazakhstan, Kyrgyzstan, Uzbekistan, Tajikistan, Pakistan and India) to conduct bilateral trade and investment in their national currencies rather than the dollar.

CRITICISMS OF THE BRI

There have been numerous criticisms of the BRI from commentators across the world. One of the most common criticisms is with regards to the debt resulting from Chinese loans for BRI projects. It is feared that this debt will create an unfavourable degree of dependency on China as a creditor. Richard Fontaine and Daniel Kliman have asserted that the BRI does not follow the international standard of debt sustainability, which may result in heavy repayment pressure on the borrowing states.[25] This would be a particular threat for small countries which would acquire high debt/GDP ratios. In this sense, Fontaine and Kliman argue, Beijing is using BRI as a China First development model. By promoting debt dependency,

China will undermine good governance and human rights in the BRI states. However, Beijing has recently responded to this criticism by promising to take into account the ability of states to service their borrowing and to offer more transparency when lending.[26]

There have been a number of other specific concerns raised regarding the BRI, most of which stem from uncertainty regarding *how* the projects will be carried out. There are major environmental concerns regarding construction projects, as a substantial investment category for China in BRI countries is in oil and gas pipelines and coal-fired power plants. China's investment in renewable energy is growing but is still much outweighed by its support for fossil fuels.[27] In 2017, the Chinese government issued a document entitled "Guidance on promoting a Green BRI," which stated in some detail how it would prioritise green development across all BRI projects. The document promises, for example, that China will promote the transfer of low-carbon technologies amongst the Belt and Road countries. Beijing has stated that the BRI infrastructure projects aim to meet five of the UN's Sustainable Development Goals, including the provision of affordable and clean energy for all.

Besides infrastructure, China is moving towards sustainability in other ways. Chinese banks have started to issue green bonds from which the proceeds are assigned only to sustainable BRI projects, and some non-infrastructure projects serve solely ecological purposes. One project underway is the China Green Foundation's extension of its existing programme of Euphrates Poplar forest restoration to countries in Central Asia. The Euphrates Poplar grows well in semi-arid conditions and would combat desertification in the region: Kyrgyzstan and Kazakhstan have both expressed interest in the project.[28] Whilst these initiatives are very welcome, it currently seems unlikely the BRI as a whole will adhere to the environmental standards needed to significantly reduce greenhouse gas emissions overall.

A further criticism is that a large proportion of the funds injected by China into recipient countries simply re-enter the Chinese system. Loans from Chinese banks are likely to be reinvested into Chinese companies—since they are more likely to win contracts—and the company will then bring a Chinese workforce to the recipient country.[29] Commentators have also complained that the concrete mechanisms needed to implement the BRI have not been fully outlined by Beijing. The academic Jie Yu points out that the official BRI document published in 2015 is essentially an advertisement of the BRI that does not set out methodologies for achieving the stated aims.[30]

A more fundamental concern for many Western commentators lies in the fear that Chinese economic influence in countries participating in the BRI, as a result of the increasing Chinese investment and financial support that will accompany the infrastructure projects, will work to Beijing's geopolitical advantage, encouraging these countries to support Beijing's self-benefitting agenda in the future. If brought to fruition, the BRI would "boost China's trade with effectively the whole Eurasian continent," and the vast trade network created would "increase the number of regional governments that view China as a patron and benefactor rather than a threat."[31] The publication Foreign Affairs predicts that through the expansion of China's ties to "major developing countries," BRI will result in a "reshaped international system that puts China at the centre of world power."[32] The BRI has also frequently been compared to the Marshall Plan enacted by the U.S. after WWII, a comparison which projects it as a strategy that will use China's economic strength to "secure foreign policy goals."[33]

The suspicion felt towards China in the governing institutions of both the United States and the European Union was reflected in their alarm at Italy's formal endorsement of the BRI in March 2019. Italy signed a memorandum of understanding expressing its support for the BRI, hoping that new investment from China would help to revive its economy.[34] Washington and Brussels, however, saw this as part of China's strategic project to gain influence and assets across the world.

Some commentators take this suspicion a step further to suggest that China has imperialist ambitions. The historian Niall Ferguson compares the Belt and Road Initiative to the Third Reich's expansionist project, warning that "President Xi Jinping has his own version of the Germans' imperial Weltpolitik."[35] This gives the impression that the Belt and Road Initiative is about territorial expansion through military means, which at present is very much not the case. Such speculation serves only to heighten fears of China unnecessarily, and diminishes the chances of international understanding and cooperation.

These observers portray China as an aggressive power devoted to projecting its geopolitical influence and shaping the economic world order to its advantage. Many of them view geopolitics as a zero-sum game: if China, or Asia more broadly, gains power and influence, others (notably the United States) will lose it. Alexander Lukin points out that this approach towards international relations stems originally from the ideas of Western political scientists such as Zbigniew Brzezinski and Samuel Huntingdon, who envisioned the world order respectively as a "grand chessboard" and a "clash of civilisations."[36]

Xi Jinping has stated that he does not subscribe to this approach: he has said that through the BRI, "we should foster a new type of international relations featuring win-win cooperation; and we should forge partnerships of dialogue with no confrontation and of friendship rather than alliance."[37] Beijing has adopted an entirely different set of principles, deliberately distinct from the Western understanding of the world order, which guide how China interacts with other nations. These are based around the idea of interdependence. The Communist Party of China (CPC) has repeatedly spoken of "jointly" building the Belt and Road in consensus with other countries. One of the goals of the Initiative is described in terms of the construction of a "community of common destiny" for all human society. A series of high-level party documents and addresses by senior leaders emphasise this. The "Vision and Actions on Jointly Building Silk Road Economic Belt and the 21st-Century Maritime Silk Road" is the first official Chinese government document on the BRI which was released jointly by three ministries of the Chinese government. In this document, the BRI is described as being designed to "uphold the global free trade regime and the open world economy in the spirit of open regional cooperation."[38]

Bruno Maçães explains that this notion of interdependence is based on the ancient Chinese concept of Tianxia, which originated roughly three thousand years ago. The central idea of Tianxia is that mutual benefit should take precedence over individual gain. As Xi said in his speech in Jakarta, "common development must be prioritised whilst seeking one's own development."[39] In light of this, Maçães has suggested that the aim of the BRI is not only to increase China's economic and geopolitical influence but to create a new world order based upon the Chinese value of interdependence. Similarly, William Callahan has suggested that the BRI, along with China's ideas of the Asian dream, the community of shared destiny, and new institutions such as the AIIB, represents China's long-term strategy to forge a comprehensive Sino-centric order covering the economic, political, cultural and security realms.[40] But observers, including Callahan himself, have admitted that China's Asia policy is still vague, and that whether China has the capacity to forge such an order is questionable, as it has some way to go to if it wants to match the US with regards to economic, military, and technological strength.[41]

The authors of this book are of the view that a narrative of the BRI as either a wholly beneficial or harmful project does not need to be sought. As mentioned, there are many legitimate concerns regarding the Initiative. Its potential impacts are uncertain and depend upon a huge number of factors, many of which are beyond China's control. Furthermore, the BRI is of massive scope and lacks clarity. It is essentially an umbrella funding mechanism for diverse projects: the academic Jie Yu observes that since the BRI's announcement, "all 31 provincial level governments from Hainan to Heilongjiang have scrambled to list their preferred projects and industries to be supported by BRI."[42] Whilst there is an overseeing body for the BRI— the "Office of the Leading Group on Promoting the Implementation of Belt and Road Initiatives"—there is currently no single department or ministry that carries the overall responsibility for it. As a result, the BRI suffers from a lack of coordination. Furthermore, almost all of China's provinces have produced their own particular BRI implementation plans. Given this, the various projects falling under the BRI are likely to result in many and varied outcomes.

Many commentators have assumed that the BRI is strategic and harmful before reaching a fuller understanding of the context in which it came about. It is this instinctive suspicion that we aim to challenge. Through the consideration of historical and present-day economic connections between China and Central Asia, this book seeks to provide a deeper understanding of the context within which BRI was conceived and is being enacted.

NEW PERSPECTIVES ON THE BRI

Whilst the authors agree that the changes planned under the BRI are of unprecedented scope and are likely to have a lasting and transformative impact, we want to emphasize that the BRI is only the most recent development in a long history of economic cooperation between China and its neighbours. Contrary to how it is usually presented, the BRI was not a brand-new initiative in 2013: a number of new projects were indeed promised, but it also brought under one umbrella several projects that were already in process. This particularly applies to Central Asia, where existing Chinese investment projects or loans have been incorporated into the BRI agenda.[43]

This book therefore contests the idea that the BRI is a *new* economic strategy. It also challenges the common assumption that China's dominant motive for undertaking the BRI is to expand its geopolitical influence. It does this by closely examining the past and present economic relationship between China and the Central Asian region. The book's focus on Central Asia of course gives a limited perspective in terms of understanding the BRI in its geographical totality, since the project extends well beyond Central Asia. However, there are already a number of books that have addressed the BRI as a whole:[44] this book's contribution is to explore the details and mechanisms of how BRI projects are being implemented within a specific regional context. Central Asia is of particular interest as it remains understudied yet is of growing importance due to its position as a gateway between China and the markets to its west in the Middle East, Africa and Europe. Central Asia also plays an important role in China's domestic policy: as discussed, Kyrgyzstan, Kazakhstan and Tajikistan all border with the westernmost Chinese province of Xinjiang. Central Asia's role in Eurasia is more important than is usually acknowledged: we emphasise in this book that the Central Asian region is not merely a group of passive actors hemmed in between larger powers but is in fact essential to the movement of goods and people across Eurasia.

Like China, the Central Asian countries have been subject to misrepresentation in English-language media. These countries are very rarely covered, and when they are, the focus is disproportionately on human rights abuses and undemocratic governance. The journalist and writer Ben Chu describes the Central Asian countries in passing as "human rights-abusing states."[45] Whilst human rights abuses absolutely must be exposed, critically discussed and fought against, they are not by any means the only thing that is going on in these countries. For example, the socio-cultural landscape of the Central Asian countries is given very little attention. Indeed, many other countries—such as the United States—have serious records of human rights abuses,[46] yet reporting does not focus solely on these, and nor should it. Central Asian countries thus appear as one-dimensionally "problematic" places. This book hopes to provide a richer, though of course in no way comprehensive, understanding of Central Asia through its exploration of the impacts of the BRI in this region.

Throughout the book, we move from giving a "macro" historical context for the region to a "micro" perspective detailing contemporary people-to-people interactions. Both approaches aim to provide a deeper understanding of the context in which the BRI is being implemented. We firstly consider the historical economic relationship and trading networks between China and Central Asia. Our account spans the whole time period from the earliest known peoples in eastern and central Asia to the present day. Chapter 1 briefly covers the majority of this period up until the incorporation of Central Asia into the Russian Empire. A particularly notable period in the history of the region was the Mongol Empire of the 13th and 14th centuries, which shaped the region significantly as it brought an unprecedented scope and intensity of economic connectivity throughout Eurasia.

In the second and third chapters, we discuss more recent economic relations, through the incorporation of Central Asia into the Russian empire and then the Soviet Union, followed by the period 1991-2013 from the end of the Soviet era up until the announcement of the BRI. The breakup of the Soviet Union resulted in the creation of five independent Central Asian states, each of which had to forge its own approach towards foreign trade: this produced both continuities and discontinuities in their economic relationships with China. Our discussion of these time periods covers illegal and informal cross-border trade as well as formal trade agreements, since both have shaped the relationship between these countries.

Any narration of the past is contested, and the events covered in the first three chapters are certainly no exception. Though we have made every effort to draw from a range of sources and perspectives, these chapters do not engage with the important debates around how to tell the stories of these times and places: rather, they aim briefly to provide a context for the BRI and to the relationship between Central Asia and China today.

This consideration of historical economic connections between China and Central Asia demonstrates that the BRI constitutes a strengthening of already-existing cooperative strategies within Eurasia. It might be better understood as a move towards something resembling the highly integrated system of trade under the Mongols. By highlighting the fact that the BRI has substantial precedents, both historical and recent, this book seeks to dispel the notions that the BRI is something new and dramatically different, and—relatedly—that the BRI is necessarily a threat.

Our second "context" for the BRI is that of people-to-people relationships between traders in Central Asia and China. The deepening of social and cultural exchanges constitutes one of the five areas China has identified through which it aims to improve connectivity between countries involved in the BRI. This aspect is rarely included in analyses of the project, however.[47] Bazaar trade became a major source of income for Central Asians after the breakup of the Soviet Union. This coincided with a rapid increase in China's economic influence in Central Asia, meaning that a large number of Central Asians have been brought into contact with the Chinese through trade as well as other activities.

Chapter 4 begins with a detailed explanation of what the key developments have been, and what is planned, under the BRI for Central Asia, looking at specific case studies of BRI projects. This is then contrasted with a study of the relationships between bazaar traders in Kyrgyzstan and Kazakhstan and their Chinese business partners. We examine how bazaar trade has shaped economic relations between these countries and China. Bazaar trade has been chosen as a site for the case studies because of the great economic significance it has acquired since the collapse of the Soviet Union in generating revenues and livelihoods, and due to its role in bringing Central Asians and Chinese into contact. The trade of bazaar goods between China and Central Asia forms a central aspect of Eurasian transnational trade; an aspect which is often ignored due to a focus by commentators on formal trade deals between nations. We take the view that the increased connectivity brought by the BRI is best understood by studying relationships at the interpersonal level as well as at the country level. We have deliberately drawn upon a case study of narrow focus, since commentary on the BRI tends to examine wider economic and geopolitical trends and overlooks their impact on the working lives and daily experiences of those affected.

A theme that runs through the history of trade in Eurasia, and which is evident in the region today, is the importance of multilateral approaches. Prajakti Kalra's work on trade in the Mongol empire demonstrates that during this time there was ongoing multilateral cooperation between the four *khans* who jointly governed Eurasia.[48] In recent years, forms of multilateral cooperation have begun to re-emerge in Asia. In 2010, a Customs Union was established between Russia, Belarus and Kazakhstan. In 2015, Kyrgyzstan and Armenia joined the union, and it was renamed the Eurasian Economic Union (EAEU). There are several other multilateral institutions in Eurasia that facilitate cooperation, including the Asian Development Bank, the Asian Infrastructure Bank, and the Shanghai Cooperation Organisation. The BRI represents a continuation of this approach: the Joint Communiqué of the Leaders Roundtable of the first Belt and Road Forum for International Cooperation calls for a strengthening of "the rules-based multilateral trading regime," and promotes "bilateral, triangular, regional and multilateral cooperation" towards a number of aims including eradicating poverty, creating jobs and promoting sustainable development.[49] Whilst statements from diplomatic proceedings will inevitably pronounce good intentions and should not be taken fully at face value, the projects that have so far been funded by the BRI are clearly in keeping with the furthering of multilateral cooperation.

The rapprochement between Russia and China in recent years has played an important role in facilitating multilateral cooperation in Eurasia. According to the scholar Alexander Lukin, each recognises the importance of the other in Central Asia: Russia sees China as a useful stabilising presence, whilst China acknowledges Russia's traditional and linguistic influence in the region.[50] Beijing is working towards developing a cooperative framework between the BRI and the regional integration initiatives proposed by Russia for the Eurasian landmass. In May 2015, Russian and Chinese leaders signed a joint statement of cooperation with the aim of linking together the EAEU and the land-based Silk Road Economic Belt. A group of Shanghai experts put together an ambitious roadmap for reaching this goal: it included coordination on infrastructure and trade, with the eventual creation of a Common Economic Space spanning all of Eurasia by 2030.[51] Beijing's pursuit of multilateral cooperation is underpinned by the afore-mentioned value framework, centring around the concept of "Tianxia," which holds that nations must be interdependent.

China's approach aligns with the British academic Andrew Gamble's recent proposal that we should prioritise the establishment and development of a multilateral international order.[52] For Gamble this is a key aspect of what he terms an "Open Left," a progressive approach that does not dogmatically adhere to any particular tradition of thought but instead aims to engage with policy ideas and intellectual movements from a wide variety of backgrounds and countries, learning from previous mistakes. An important component of Gamble's approach is that non-Western actors be enabled to play a greater role in rule-making processes than they formerly have. As Gamble observes, the international order established after 1945 "reflected US priorities and interests."[53] Recent years have seen increasing fragmentation in Europe and America, with resistance by populist movements and political leaders against participation in a multilateral order. This is in contrast to the overall trend towards economic and political cooperation in Asia.

This is further reason not to regard the BRI with immediate suspicion, but rather with curiosity. An understanding of the historical cooperation between China and Central Asia may suggest to us possibilities for new forms of international order today.

The vast majority of this book was written before the Covid-19 pandemic. As a result, it does not cover China or Central Asia's responses to this in any depth. However, the importance of international cooperation, and the problems that arise from a lack of it, have been starkly highlighted by recent events. Given this, the authors believe that the themes of this book are deeply relevant to the ongoing public health crisis.

NOTES

1. Khanna, P. (2019). *The future is Asian: global order in the twenty-first century*. Simon & Schuster.

2. Maçães, B. (2018). *Belt and road: A Chinese world order*. Hurst & Company.

3. Chongyang Institute for Financial Studies. (Ed). (2014). *The Eurasian era: blue book of Silk Road economic study*. Renmin University of China.

4. See e.g. Lukin, A. (2019). Russian–Chinese Cooperation in Central Asia and the Idea of Greater Eurasia. India Quarterly: A Journal of International Affairs, 75(1), 1–14.

5. Abu-Lughod, J. (1991). *Before European hegemony: The world system A.D. 1250-1350*. New York: Oxford University Press, p. 159.

6. Fang, C., & Nolan, P. (Ed). (2019). *Handbook of the Belt and Road*. New York: Routledge

7. Chongyang Institute for Financial Studies, The Eurasian era, p. 23.

8. Bin, M. (2020). Rhetoric vs reality in China's BRI: a case study of China Railway Express. Lecture, Cambridge University.

9. For examples of China's energy projects, see Columbia University, "Guide to Chinese Climate Policy." Retrieved from https://chineseclimate policy.energypolicy.columbia.edu/en/energy-sector-projects#/_ftn7

10. Maçães, *Belt and road*, p. 32.

11. Miner, S. (2016). Economic and Political Implications. In Djankov, S. et al. (2016). China's Belt and Road Initiative: Motive, Scope and Challenges. The Peterson Institution for International Economics. Briefing 16–2, p. 12.

12. Sanderson, H. (2017, September 26). BHP says China's Belt and Road plan could require 150m tonnes of steel. Financial Times. Retrieved from https://www.ft.com/content/5ec23b24-4f0c-3729-b1b0-41aef3427e1b.

13. Miner, Economic and Political Implications, in China's Belt and Road Initiative, p. 12.

14. Wu, H. (2015, December 29). Bankers behind "Belt and Road" business surge. Retrieved from http://english.caixin.com/2015-12-29/100893993.html

15. Ferdinand, P. (2016). Westward ho—the China dream and "one belt, one road": Chinese foreign policy under Xi Jinping. International Affairs, 92(4), 941–957.

16. Hu, A. (2008). Zhongguo: min sheng yu fazhan [China: people's livelihood and development. Beijing: Zhongguo jingji, pp. 99–117.

17. China Statistical Yearbook. (2014). Beijing: China Statistics Press, 2014, table 6-20. Retrieved from http://www.stats.gov.cn/tjsj/ ndsj/2014/ indexeh.htm

18. Ferdinand, Westward ho.

19. Callahan, W. A. (2016). China's "Asia Dream": The Belt Road Initiative and the new regional order. Asian Journal of Comparative Politics, 1(3), 226–243.

20. Fallon, T. (2015). The New Silk Road: Xi Jinping's Grand Strategy for Eurasia, American Foreign Policy Interests, 37(3), 140–147.

21. Lain, S. (2018). The Potential and Pitfalls of Connectivity along the Silk Road Economic Belt. In Laruelle, M. (Ed). China's belt and road initiative and its impact in central Asia. George Washington University, Central Asia Program.

22. Wang, H., & Lu, M. (2016). *China goes global: The impact of Chinese overseas investment on its business enterprises.* Basingstoke: Palgrave Macmillan, p. 174.

23. See e.g. Djankov, S. et al, China's Belt and Road Initiative.

24. Tsui, S., Erebus, W., Lau, K. C., & Tiejun, W. (2017). One belt, one road: China's strategy for a new global financial order. Monthly Review, 68(8), 36–45.

25. Fontaine, R., & Kliman, D. (2018, May 15). On China's New Silk Road, Democracy pays a toll. Retrieved from https://foreignpolicy.com/2018/05/16/on-chinas-new-silk-road-democracy-pays-a-toll/

26. Hornby, L. (2019, April 25). China pledges to address debt worries over Belt and Road. Financial Times. Retrieved from https://www.ft.com/content/f7442058-66f9-11e9-9adc-98bf1d35a056

27. Climate Home News. (2019, April 25). China promotes "Green" Belt and Road, but is pressured over coal investments. Retrieved from https://www.climatechangenews.com/2019/04/25/china-promotes-green-belt-road-pressured-coal-investments/

28. Wang, Y. (2019, Jan). Greening the Desert. China Report, vol no. 68.

29. Laruelle, China's Belt and Road Initiative, p. X.

30. Yu, J. (2018). The belt and road initiative: domestic interests, bureaucratic politics and the EU-China relations. Asia Europe Journal, 16(3).

31. Tiezzi, S. (2014, November 6). The New Silk Road: China's Marshall Plan. The Diplomat. Retrieved from https://thediplomat.com/2014/11/the-new-silk-road-chinas-marshall-plan/

32. Stokes, J. (2015, April 19). China's Road Rules. Foreign Affairs. Retrieved from https://www.foreignaffairs.com/articles/asia/2015-04-19/chinas-road-rules

33. Tiezzi, The New Silk Road.

34. Ghiglione, D. et al. (2019, March 6). Italy set to formally endorse China's Belt and Road Initiative. Financial Times.

35. Ferguson, N. (2018). "As Trump and Xi spar, an ancient trap awaits both". Retrieved from http://www.niallferguson.com/journalism/politics/as-trump-and-xi-spar-an-ancient-trap-awaits-both

36. Lukin, A. (2019). Russian–Chinese Cooperation in Central Asia and the Idea of Greater Eurasia. India Quarterly, 75(1), 1–14, p. 7.

37. Yamei. (Ed). (2017, May 14). Full text of President Xi's speech at opening of Belt and Road forum, Xinhua News. Retrieved from http://www.xinhuanet.com//english/2017-05/14/c_136282982.htm

38. National Development and Reform Commission, Ministry of Foreign Affairs and Ministry of Commerce of the People's Republic of China with State Council Authorization (NDRC MFA and MOC). (2015). Vision and actions on jointly building Silk Road Economic Belt and 21st-Century Maritime Silk Road. Retrieved from http://en.ndrc.gov.cn/newsrelease/201503/t20150330_669367.html

39. Maçaes, *Belt and Road*, p. 28.

40. Callahan, China's "Asia Dream."

41. Callahan. Also see Jakobson, L. (2016). Reflections from China on Xi Jinping's "Asia for Asians." Asian Politics & Policy, 8(1), 219–223.

42. Yu, J. (2018). The belt and road initiative: Domestic interests, bureaucratic politics and the EU-China relations. Asia Europe Journal, 16(3), 223–236, p. 225.

43. Lain, The Potential and Pitfalls of Connectivity, p. 1.

44. See e.g. Frankopan, P. (2018). *The New Silk Roads: The Present and Future of the World.* London: Bloomsbury Publishing, Khanna, *The Future is Asian,* and Maçaes, *Belt and Road.*

45. Chu, B. (2013). *Chinese whispers: why everything you've heard about China is wrong.* London: Weidenfeld & Nicholson, p. 200.

46. See e.g. Bevins, V. (2020). *The Jakarta Method: Washington's Anticommunist Crusade and the Mass Murder Program That Shaped Our World.* New York: Public Affairs.

47. Exceptions include Sadovskaya, Y. & Utyasheva, L. (2018). "Human Silk Road": The People-to-People Aspect of the Belt and Road Initiative. In (Ed). Laruelle, M. China's Belt and Road Initiative and its impact in Central Asia. Washington D.C.: The George Washington University, Central Asia Program.

48. Kalra, P. (2018). *The Silk Road and the Political Economy of the Mongol Empire.* Routledge Studies on the Chinese Economy.

49. China Daily. (2017, May 16). Joint Communiqué of the Leaders Roundtable of the Belt and Road Forum for International Cooperation. Retrieved from https://www.chinadaily.com.cn/china/2017-05/16/content_29359366.htm

50. Lukin, Russian-Chinese cooperation in Central Asia, p. 3.

51. Ibid, p. 7.

52. Gamble, A. (2018). Open Left: The Future of Progressive Politics. London: Rowman & Littlefield.

53. Gamble, Open Left, p. 5.

Chapter I

A HISTORY OF ECONOMIC CONNECTIONS ACROSS THE ASIAN LANDMASS

In dominant historical narratives, events in Europe and America have tended to take centre stage. This has obscured transformative developments in Asia, as well as ƒthe emergence of important connections across the whole Eurasian continent. The history of Central Asia in particular is little understood. Its very centrality within the Eurasian landmass makes it both important—as a region connecting different parts of Eurasia—and frequently overlooked, since it has often been subsumed into larger empires.[1]

There have, however, been many alternative global histories written from Asian and/or Eurasian perspectives, with some in recent years aiming to reach a wide readership beyond academia.[2] This chapter builds on these valuable contributions, focussing specifically on the history of interaction between China and the peoples of the region we would now term "Central Asia." We begin with the earliest known societies in the region and end with Central Asia's nineteenth-century incorporation into the Russian and Chinese empires, since this resulted in the first impermeable border to be drawn across the region. History gives us the necessary context for understanding the connections, economic and otherwise, between the two regions today. Furthermore, the different ways in which past societies organised themselves provide alternative conceptualisations of power and governance in the region, posing a challenge to dominant understandings of Asian geopolitics. The Mongol Empire, as we will argue, is an especially pertinent example of this.

In contemporary usage, the term "Central Asia" usually refers to the five former Soviet republics: Kazakhstan, Turkmenistan, Uzbekistan, Tajikistan and Kyrgyzstan. However, these republics were delineated in the early years of the Soviet era and, inevitably, the borders are somewhat arbitrary. Furthermore, as a landlocked region, Central Asia has always been heavily influenced by its neighbours and has seen numerous major ethnic migrations.[3] The political geography, culture and ethnic makeup of the region therefore involve areas well beyond the five former Soviet republics. Historically, there was never an all-embracing term for the Central Asian region. The UNESCO History of the Civilizations of Central Asia defines the area as "Afghanistan, north-eastern Iran, northern and central Pakistan, northern India, western China, Mongolia and the former Soviet Central Asia republics," involving the "vast area extending from the Caspian Sea to the high plateau of Mongolia."[4] On the other hand, there are some natural boundaries that delimit the region geographically: to the West, the area is bounded by the Caspian Sea and to the East by the Tian Shan and Pamir mountains. The steppe, which is Central Asia's dominant ecological zone, also sets the region apart from others. It consists of a mixture of prairie, desert and semi-desert, punctuated by oases.[5] The features of the steppe ecosystem gave rise to a particular kind of society: the nomadic peoples. Nonetheless, the steppe is not confined to Central Asia. In order to recognise the ambiguity of Central Asia's geographical delimitations, our account of the region and its historical interaction with China understands Central Asia as consisting of peoples and civilisations rather than as a defined geographical area.

NOMADIC AND SEDENTARY PEOPLES

The earliest known ancestors of steppe peoples were the Indo-European linguistic community, who inhabited the Black Sea steppes. They began to disperse around 3000–2500 BC, producing groups moving into central and south Asia and the northern Mediterranean. One group, the Indo-Iranians, went eastward to Siberia, Mongolia, Xinjiang and northern Pakistan, becoming the ancestors of the Indic-speaking populations in South Asia and Iranian-speaking populations of Iran and Central Asia today.[6] On the vast grassy plains of the steppe, they learned to domesticate horses and breed livestock, becoming pastoral nomads by 2000 BC. The nomads later combined their horsemanship with wheeled carts and archery, and had begun to develop disciplined cavalry by 1000 BC.[7]

By the eighth century BC, there existed two distinct zones of civilization in Central Asia. To the north of the Tian Shan, Altai and Caucasus mountain ranges lived the Iranian nomadic tribes, called the Scythians by the Greeks and the Sakas by the Persians. The steppe supported their cattle-breeding economy. These tribes "presided over a vast trading network linking Greeks, Persians, and Indians" whilst also carrying out raids on settled societies.[8] To the south, other Iranian farmers settled in the oases and fertile valleys, forming the Sogdian and Khwarazmian peoples in modern-day Uzbekistan, and the Bactrians in Afghanistan. Still others, such as the Khotanese Saka, went further east and established themselves in a number of the oasis city-states in modern-day Xinjiang.[9] Central Asia thus became a space in which nomadic and sedentary peoples coexisted.

In the sixth century BC, some of the regions in Central Asia, such as Margiana (modern-day Turkmenistan), Sogdia, Khwarazm and Bactria, became part of the expanding Persian (Achaemenid) Empire. This was a vast state stretching from the shores of the Aegean Sea, southwards to Egypt and eastwards to the Himalayas.[10] The Persians constructed over 1600 miles of road network, linking the coast of Asia Minor with Babylon, Susa and Persepolis. The transportation system brought Central Asia into transcontinental commerce with the states to its west, and this road network later became a central link in the Silk Road.[11]

The above period also witnessed the development of Chinese civilization in the region to the east of Central Asia, from prehistory to the early imperial period. Agriculture became widespread in China around 4000 BC.[12] The earliest known dynasty for which there is archaeological evidence is the Shang from 1700 to 1027 BC, under which bronze was manufactured. The Zhou dynasty which followed in the first millennium BC saw China engaging in occasional trade both with nomads to its north and sedentary peoples to its west.[13] In 221 BC, the first imperial state of China—the Qin dynasty—was established through the conquest and unification of six other warring states by the Qin state. Its boundary extended "in the north to the Great Wall, the southern boundary line of present-day Inner Mongolia, and the Jade Gate in Gansu province, in the west to the foothills of the Himalayas and the basin of the Salween River and in the south to the border of modern Vietnam."[14]

The earliest production of silk took place in China during this time. Archaeological research has found weaving implements and dyed silk gauzes dating to 3600 BC in Hemudu, Zhejiang province, which is still one of the main silk-producing centres today in China. Farmers grew mulberry trees, using their leaves to feed silkworms. Weavers extracted silk fibre from the cocoons, spun silk yarn, and wove silk textiles. Chinese silk came to be considered a luxury trade item by nomadic and sedentary peoples in Central Asia, as well as by those in the Mediterranean region.

THE DEVELOPMENT OF THE SILK ROAD

In the third century BC, a powerful nomadic confederacy named Xiongnu emerged on the Mongolian grassland, living on the northwestern border of China and within the eastern part of what is now Central Asia. The nomadic shepherds were in perpetual conflict with their sedentary farming neighbours and became China's chief enemy during the Qin (221–206 BC) and Han (206 BC–220 AD) dynasties. The emperor of the Qin dynasty ordered the construction of a grand fortification, the Great Wall, based on remaining fortifications along the empire's northern frontier, and used the wall as military defence in its wars with Xiongnu raids.[15] Following a crushing defeat by the Xiongnu around 200 BC, the Han dynasty appeased them by paying substantial amounts of silk to them as an annual tribute.[16]

There were also some smaller states scattered in the basins and along the foothills of the Tian Shan and Altai Mountains in modern-day Xinjiang, which served as tributary states for Xiongnu, providing agricultural products, taxes, and labour to the nomadic confederation. West of the Xiongnu territory lived the Yuezhi people, another rival of the Xiongnu, who maintained friendly trading relations with agricultural China. Around 130 BC, the Xiongnu fought and defeated the Yuezhi, who fled from their homeland and migrated across the pastures north of the Tian Shan range all the way to Bactria.

Meanwhile in China, Emperor Wudi of the Han, ruling from 141–87 BC, presided over a considerable expansion of Chinese territory. He proposed joint action with the nomadic tribes against their common enemy, the Xiongnu. When he heard the news that the Yuezhi had been defeated by the Xiongnu, he sent an envoy named Zhang Qian to the Yuezhi to enlist their support. On his way to the Yuezhi, Zhang Qian had to pass through Xiongnu territory and was detained there for ten years. When he at last encountered the Yuezhi, he failed to persuade them into allying with the Han, and eventually returned to the Han court in 126 BC.

Despite failing in its diplomatic mission, Zhang Qian's trip was a valuable one for China. Zhang Qian was the first Chinese person to travel through the "western regions," as Central Asia was known at that time in China. Prior to his trip, Central Asia had been known only as a mythical land mentioned in Chinese legends. Zhang Qian brought back detailed information about the steppe and the trading habits and resources of the settlements he encountered. His knowledge of the region drew great attention in the Han court. For example, in Bactria, he had noticed that objects made of bamboo and cloth manufactured in Southern China were being sold.[17] He surmised that the peoples of the western regions were keen to acquire Han goods, and proposed to the emperor that it would be possible to win them over using the Han's economic influence.

One of the western goods which aroused the greatest interest for the Han emperor was the horse. At that time, horses could not be bred successfully in China, and those imported from Mongolia were just "shaggy, furry little creatures," unlike the splendid Arab steeds of the western regions.[18] Horses were seen as being of great importance for military matters, as the superiority of cavalry over infantry had been amply demonstrated by the Xiongnu. Zhang Qian introduced the emperor to the horse-breeding groups in Central Asia, including the Yuezhi, the Wusun (nomads of the Ili valley to the south of Lake Balkash) and the Dawan (inhabitants of Ferghana). These encounters provided further motivation as well as military intelligence for the Han Empire's expansion towards the west. The most famous and valuable mounts were bred in Dawan, and were distinguished for their strength: they were named "heavenly" horses by Emperor Wudi and were often associated with dragons—an indication of how greatly valued they were, given the dragon's elevated status in Chinese culture.[19]

The Han campaign against the Xiongnu continued. China took control of the Gansu corridor and later even extended its campaigns as far as Ferghana, beyond the Pamir mountains.[20] As a result, the kingdoms to the west in the Tarim basin (in today's Xinjiang) were brought under the tributary system of Han China. In some states, the Han set up new official posts and occasionally appointed Han people as officials. To secure China's access to the routes leading to the western regions, Wudi had the Great Wall extended north-westward all the way to the Jade Gate, the westernmost garrison town, near Dunhuang. He then set up a system of garrisons all along this part of the Great Wall.

This relatively safe route attracted foreign merchants to enter China and sell Chinese goods back to Central Asia and West Asia as far as the Mediterranean Sea. The eastern end of the trade route was Chang' an, the capital of Han China. Traders heading west from Chang'an would go through the Gansu corridor, which runs east to west between the Qinghai Mountains to the south and the Gobi Desert of Mongolia to the north. After reaching the oasis city of Dunhuang in Gansu, travellers had to pass through the Tarim basin, the low-lying desert between the Pamir mountains to the west and Lop Nor, a salt lake, to the east. The westernmost end of the route was the Amu Darya river.[21]

The importation of horses from Central Asia was a major feature of all Han treaties with the western regions. Central Asian furs were also transported into China, as were other goods from distant locations: in the city of Chang'an, Roman glassware and Indian textiles could be found. And, of course, one of the most sought-after trade goods was silk, common in China but internationally seen as a luxury textile.

Ancient traders had no word for this network of routes existing between China and the Mediterranean. The term "Silk Road," originally *die Seidenstrasse*, was coined in 1877 by a German geographer of China, Baron Ferdinand von Richthofen, as a reference to the enduring value and power of silk during that period. At the time, Germany had colonial interests in eastern China, and Richthofen was trying to promote the construction of a commercial railway from China to Europe: the idea of there being a single "road" was therefore a product of this colonial vision of China.[22] This term was increasingly adopted and is now used by China to describe its own history. However, the term is somewhat misleading, as in reality there were multiple and shifting trade routes, and there were many other items traded besides silk.

Silk from China found a particularly large market in the Roman Empire. The Romans connected with the Central Asian section of the Silk Road through ports in Barygaza, a city in western India (now Bharuch). They spent huge sums of money on the importation of this luxury good. Notably, most of the Roman Empire's spending on silk went into the pockets of the intermediaries along the Silk Road rather than to China. Trade was predominantly conducted by these intermediaries rather than by direct interaction between the Chinese and the Romans. Central Asians therefore played a crucial role in bringing about the movement of goods from China to Europe.

A number of empires and peoples, both nomadic and sedentary, based in the Central Asian region were instrumental in controlling trade across Eurasia. From the mid-first to mid-third century AD, a strategic portion of the Silk Road came to be controlled by the Kushan empire. This empire had arisen from one of the five constituent tribes of the Yuezhi. The Kushans' territory included Bactria in present-day Afghanistan, Ferghana, and an area to the west of the Tarim Basin in present-day Pakistan, through which most Chinese goods were exported. The Kushan empire expanded southwards as far as the mouth of the Indus, thereby controlling the maritime trade route that directly connected India with the Roman ports in Egypt. Goods transported by this trade route included silk from China and turquoise, lapis lazuli, and animal furs from Afghanistan and Central Asia. Alongside the Kushans' role in enabling commercial flow, they also brought Buddhism into Central Asia and China.[23]

The Sogdians, an Iranian people who inhabited the fertile valleys flanked by the Amu and Syr rivers, were also prominent traders, and after the fall of the Kushan empire became even more so. From the second century BC until the end of the Tang dynasty (tenth century AD), they had a significant presence on the trade routes, mediating between nomads, oasis dwellers, and sedentary empires. Their homeland was the fortified city of Marakanda, now Samarkand. It lay at a strategically important point along the Silk Road, near the intersection between the east-west route and the north-south highway between India and Russia.[24] The Sogdians were responsible for transporting grapevines and alfalfa to China to feed the "heavenly" horses from Ferghana, and they also transported luxury items from the states at the western end of the Silk Road, such as Sassanian silverware from Persia, glass vessels and beads from Syria and Babylon, Mediterranean coral, and purple woollen cloth from Rome. The transmission of paper-making technology to Europe was facilitated by the Sogdians, who learned paper-making from China and established it in Samarkand in the eighth century.[25] The Sogdian's Iranian language became the common language among traders in Central Asia up until the Arab conquests in the eighth century.[26]

It was not only goods and people that moved along the Silk Roads, but also religions and ideas. With the expansion of the Sassanian empire (the last kingdom of the Persian empire) into Sogdia, many Sogdian traders adopted Zoroastrianism or Manichaeism.[27] Buddhism was also introduced to the Sogdians: the Yuezhi had encountered it from the Ganges valley to their south, and brought it into Central Asia.[28] Sogdian merchants and travellers disseminated these religions along the Silk Roads and eastwards to China. Asia thus developed a rich cultural connectivity.

In the fourth century AD, a confederation of Turkic and Iranian peoples from northern Afghanistan, the Hephthalites, emerged as a superpower in the Eurasian continent. Although they were new to trade, they minted silver coins based on Kushan standards, and encouraged trade to continue.[29] In the meantime, the Roman Empire transited to the Byzantine Empire, becoming a greater consumer and producer of silk than its predecessor. The Byzantines established their own sophisticated silk weaving industry under state monopoly, meaning that by the fifth and sixth centuries, China was no longer the sole producer of silk textiles. The Byzantines, Persians and Sogdians imported Chinese silk yarn as raw material and China bought silk textiles from the Byzantines along with other goods.

552 AD saw a major Turkic tribal confederation enter the scene: the Göktürks formed a Turkic Khanate, which spread across much of Central Asia and today's Mongolia. Following this, Turkic Khanates continued to reign in Central Asia for several centuries. Notably, these included the Uyghur Khanate, which lasted from 744–840 AD and was one of the largest states to emerge during the medieval era in Eurasia: it was centred on the Mongolian steppe, but at its height

reached from western Central Asia to Korea.[30] Whilst the Uyghurs were pastoral nomads, they took on several features typically seen as belonging to sedentary societies, such as agriculture, a written alphabet and the adoption of a state religion (Manichaeism). Many of these features were adopted due to the Uyghurs' close trading relationships with Tang China and the Sogdians.[31]

Arab conquests in the eighth century AD brought a shift from the Sogdian language to Farsi, and to a new religion, Islam.[32] This resulted in major conversions of Turkic tribes and the emergence of the first Turkic Muslim empire, the Karakhanid Khanate, which in the mid-tenth century declared Islam to be its state religion.[33] At this time in China, the Tang dynasty was becoming a distinctly cosmopolitan empire, welcoming large number of merchants including Arabs and Persians, some of whom were invited to settle permanently in Chinese cities.[34] The cities of Dunhuang, Gaochang and Turfan, in the northwest of modern China, were all vibrant and important localities for trade.

Despite the waxing and waning of numerous kingdoms along the Silk Road, trade continued with the coming and going of different players and the increasing diversification of traded goods. As Hasan Karrar points out, the existence of Silk Road trade depended fundamentally upon the ability of Inner Asians to "adapt to changing circumstances through mobility" within the inhospitable landscape of the steppe.[35]

Central Asians, and the empires and confederations of which they were a part, played an enduringly vital role in trade. But it was under the Mongol Empire in the thirteenth and fourteenth centuries that Eurasia reached unprecedented levels of connectedness and prosperity.

THE MONGOL EMPIRE AND
THIRTEENTH-CENTURY MULTILATERALISM

Following a period of instability and shifting allegiances in Inner Asia, the Mongol leader Genghis Khan brought together tribes in northeast Asia and led military campaigns across Eurasia, conquering Central Asia between 1218 and 1220. Earlier in Genghis Khan's life, he and his family had been abandoned by their tribe and subsequently had been forced to live with constant insecurity, experiencing kidnappings by other tribes.[36] As a result, Genghis wanted to create stability on the steppe by uniting it under one leader and ending the ongoing tribal warfare. A series of conquests gave rise to an empire which, under his rule, stretched from the Caspian Sea to the East Sea (the Sea of Japan).[37]

The conquests continued following Genghis Khan's death in 1227, and the empire was at its largest after Khubilai Khan, the grandson of Genghis Khan, conquered Southern China in 1279. At this point, the empire extended all the way to modern-day Hungary and Poland in the west, to the northern borders of Burma and India in the south and into Russia and Siberia in the north (Fig. 1.1). China was thus directly connected to Europe under the Mongols. The Mongol Empire was the largest continuous land empire ever to have existed, and the period of Mongol rule was the only time in history during which the entire Silk Road was united under one political system.

The Mongol expansion has been described as "the first global event"[38] and "a golden moment in the history of Eurasian trade."[39] The Mongols set up a number of institutions to encourage trade across the empire, since they placed a high value on trade and prioritised its facilitation. This was an approach which stemmed from the fact that they were a nomadic people. Trade along the Silk Road had traditionally experienced a number of limitations, which the Mongols were able to overcome.[40] The chief problem was that the empire spanned huge political, religious and ethnic differences. The numerous and diverse peoples along the Silk Road meant that security was vital for trade: in the absence of protection, traders were at permanent risk of being plundered. The Mongols installed *tamamci* (garrison troops) in all areas of the empire in order to ensure safety for merchants. They regularised taxes across the empire: this "made transport costs calculable," whereas previously it had been impossible for merchants to predict how much a journey would cost.[41] Alongside this, they set up the first postal system to connect the whole Eurasian realm, allowing messages to travel vast distances, and created the necessary financial infrastructure for commerce. Trade was facilitated through the establishment of manufacturing workshops in close proximity to physical markets. Amenities for merchants, such as rest stations supplying fresh horses, were provided. These were particularly important given that the arid steppe terrain presented a difficult environment for foreign travellers: medieval European merchants describing the steppe complained of "weeks of travel with no resources to draw on."[42] Traders from all religious and ethnic backgrounds were made to feel welcome, and merchants occupied an elevated social status across the empire.[43]

The diversity of peoples across Eurasia also presented a challenge for Mongol governance. By 1260, the Mongol empire was divided into four states, known as Khanates: Yuan China, Ilkhanate Persia, Chagatai Central Asia and the Golden Horde (Fig. 1.1). Each Khanate had its own ruler, or Khan. The Mongols governed with

Figure 1.1.   The Four Khanates of the Mongol Empire. Source: https://commons.wikimedia.org/wiki/File:Division_of_Mongol_Empire.jpg

a remarkable tolerance for alternative ways of life, as their ideology allowed for pluralism of religion and culture. They enforced a shared political system, but without undermining the wide variety of existing local structures across Eurasia. Their administration can therefore be understood as a "suprastructure."[44] In some areas, such as in the Uyghur kingdom and Ferghana, the Mongols allowed local dynasties to remain in place, as long as they were subservient to the Khan.[45] The academic Prajakti Kalra observes that all spheres of administration were subject to the combining of Mongol and local elements.[46] Governments were made up of a mixture of personnel: in Yuan China, both Muslims and non-Muslims from Central Asia held important governmental roles, such as generals and in central financial administration.[47] At Karakorum, the capital of the Mongol empire for some time, there were Uyghur advisors who would provide expertise in the language and culture of Central Asia.[48] Crucially, though, there were common features between Khanates, such as the legal code, the economic institutions mentioned above and the appointment of Mongols in key political positions. This ensured political and economic unity across the empire whilst preserving existing differences between societies.

The Mongols did not have to resort to total centralisation in order to maintain this unity. The Khans of different states interacted with one another in a manner that we would now describe as multilateral cooperation. Such cooperation was built upon Mongol and nomadic ideologies, such as openness towards different religions, and the belief in the centrality of trade.

This multilateral approach offers an alternative for the Central Asian states today who fear being dominated by larger powers in the region. As Kalra points out, this fear comes to a great extent from particular ideas about power generated within Europe's colonial past; ideas which have their origins outside of Central Asia.[49] A multilateral approach to governance is much better suited to Eurasia, a region which, due to its geography and continual migratory movements, has an innate connectedness.

THE DECLINE OF THE SILK ROAD

The Mongol empire's connectivity also had undesirable consequences: it facilitated the spread of a great plague across Eurasia, which left many dead, inhibited trade along the Silk Road and contributed to the breakdown of the empire.[50] Internal unrest enabled regions within the empire to be reclaimed by other powers. The Mongols left a fragmented legacy, some parts of which endured longer than others. The Mongol-led Yuan dynasty collapsed in 1368 and was replaced by the Ming dynasty. In Central Asia, Amir Timur (also known as Tamerlane), who was Turkic-speaking, Muslim, and claimed to be a descendant of Genghis Khan, took control of the Chagatai Khanate. This gave rise to the Timurid empire, which lasted until 1507. A descendant of Timur, Babur, was the first of a succession of Mughal[51] rulers whose territory included the Ferghana valley and most of the Indian subcontinent.[52] The last nomadic empire left over from the Mongols was the Dzungar khanate of the seventeenth and eighteenth centuries, which encompassed modern-day Xinjiang and parts of Kazakhstan and Kyrgyzstan. Between 1750 and 1757, China annexed the area, killing much of the population. With the defeat of the Dzungars, Xinjiang came under Chinese rule.

This period also saw the beginnings of Russian expansion into Central Asia, which was hitherto unprecedented. Between 1680 and 1760, Kazakh tribes faced attacks from Dzungars to their east and sought protection from Russia. As a consequence, most of the Kazakh tribes had been incorporated into the Russian empire by the early nineteenth century.[53] In the second half of the nineteenth century, Russia expanded into the rest of Central Asia, taking the city of Tashkent in 1865, Samarkand in 1868, and the khanates of Khiva, Khokand and Bukhara.

With the expansion of European exploration by sea from the fifteenth century onwards, new maritime trade routes emerged, which lessened the importance of the land-bound silk roads across Eurasia. According to the academic Xinru Liu, the demand for porcelain also contributed to the growth in maritime trade as it could not be easily transported by land caravan.[54] With their growing military and ship-building expertise, Europeans then began to colonise numerous parts of Asia. In China, Europeans seized ports, such as those in Shanghai and Hong Kong. Britain's colonisation of India brought implications for Central Asia, as the British hoped to use the region to prevent Russia from accessing India. A diplomatic confrontation known as the "Great Game" ensued for much of the nineteenth century, until the two powers agreed in 1893 to keep Afghanistan as a buffer state—though by this point Central Asia had become incorporated into the Russian empire.

European expansionism thus played an important part in curtailing the thriving trade networks across Asia that had operated for millennia. In the early twentieth century, a number of Asian intellectuals wrote about the long history of linkages across Asia, including between Chinese and Muslims, and bemoaned the fact that European colonialism had "severed Asia's historical interconnectivity."[55] By the nineteenth century, the whole of Inner Asia had come under a combination of Russian and Chinese jurisdictions, both of which were sedentary powers with modernising ambitions. Prior to this, no centralising state had existed in Central Asia: there had never been a ruling elite who had deliberately set out to transform the social fabric of the region.[56] The encroachment of Russian and Chinese sedentary states in the eighteenth and nineteenth centuries meant that the region encompassing Central Asia and China lost the fluidity it had retained since ancient times.

It is clear from this brief summary of Central Asia's history that the region long played a crucial role in the global economy. Central Asians were indispensable to the movement of goods across Eurasia and therefore to the economic prosperity of numerous peoples and regions. Prior to European colonial expansion, Europe remained largely peripheral to the thriving Asian trading network.

This chapter has also shown that Asia has a long history of multipolarity and interconnection. There is a deep shared heritage connecting Central Asia and China. The Silk Road witnessed the continuous flow of capital, technology, goods, people and religion.

This suggests that the region, and Asia more broadly, can achieve a similar level of cooperation again. And indeed, this process may be underway. Hundreds of years after the Silk Road prospered, a modern Eurasian integration project—the Belt and Road Initiative—aims to build on the cultural aspiration of the ancient Silk Road. However, this project faces many new obstacles that the Silk Road did not. In order to understand these obstacles, we must firstly look more closely at how the rise of the Chinese and Russian empires created barriers within the region, and at how the Central Asian region was subsumed into Sino-Soviet relations.

NOTES

1. Cummings, S. N. (2012). *Understanding Central Asia: politics and contested transformations.* New York: Routledge, p. 1.
2. For academic publications see e.g. Abu-Lughod, J. (1991). *Before European hegemony: The world system A.D. 1250–1350.* New York: Oxford University Press and Kalra, P. (2018). *The Silk Road and the Political Economy of the Mongol Empire.* Routledge Studies on the Chinese Economy. For publications reaching a wider audience see e.g. Frankopan, P. (2015). *The silk roads: a new history of the world.* London: Bloomsbury Publishing and Khanna, P. (2019). *The future is Asian: global order in the twenty-first century.* Simon & Schuster.
3. Cummings, *Understanding Central Asia*, p. 2.
4. Harmatta, J., Puri, B. N., & Etemadi, G. F. (Ed). (1994). *History of civilizations of Central Asia: volume II: The development of sedentary and nomadic civilizations: 700 BC to AD 250.* Paris: UNESCO, p. 7.
5. Golden, P. B. (2011). *Central Asia in world history.* New York: Oxford University Press, p. 4.
6. J. P. Mallory, D. Q. Adams. (2006). *The oxford introduction to Proto-Indo-European and the Proto-Indo-European world.* New York: Oxford University Press, p. 34.
7. Golden, *Central Asia in World History*, pp. 9–12.
8. Khanna, *The Future is Asian,* p. 29.
9. Golden, *Central Asia in World History,* p. 24.
10. Frankopan, P. (2015). *The silk roads: A new history of the world.* London: Bloomsbury Publishing, p. 1.

11. Golden, *Central Asia in World History,* p. 16.

12. Ibid.

13. Khanna, *The Future is Asian,* p. 30.

14. Meskill, J. T. (1973). *An introduction to Chinese civilization.* Lexington: D C Heath & Co, pp. 3–37.

15. Di Cosmo, N., & American Council of Learned Societies. (2004). *Ancient China and its enemies the rise of nomadic power in East Asian history (ACLS Humanities E-Book).* Cambridge, UK ; New York: Cambridge University Press, p. 152–155.

16. Di Cosmo, N., & American Council of Learned Societies. p. 192.

17. Hansen, V. (2012). *The Silk Road: a new history.* New York: Oxford University Press, p. 14.

18. Coates, A. (1994). *China Races.* Hong Kong: Oxford University Press, p. 23.

19. Wood, F. (2002). *The Silk Road: two thousand years in the heart of Asia.* Berkeley, Calif: University of California Press, p. 55.

20. Liu, *The Silk Road in world history,* p.10.

21. Whitfield, S. (2015). *Life Along the Silk Road.* Berkeley, Calif: University of California Press, p. 2.

22. See Chin, T. (2013). The Invention of the Silk Road, 1877. Critical Inquiry, 40(1), 194–219.

23. Liu, *The Silk Road in world history,* pp. 21–48.

24. Abu-Lughod, *Before European hegemony,* p. 178.

25. Wood, *The Silk Road,* p. 69.

26. Liu, *The Silk Road in world history,* p. 68.

27. Ibid, pp. 68–73.

28. Khanna, *The Future is Asian,* p. 32.

29. Liu, *The Silk Road in world history,* p. 85.

30. Kovalev, R. K. (2016). Uyghur Khanate. *The Encyclopedia of Empire,* 1–6.

31. Gladney, D. C. (1998). Internal colonialism and the Uyghur nationality: Chinese nationalism and its subaltern subjects. *Cahiers d'Etudes sur la Méditerranée Orientale et le monde Turco-Iranien,* (25).

32. Cummings, *Understanding Central Asia,* p. 24.

33. Xia, W. (2017, June). The Review of the Buddhism History and Culture in Kashgar. In *2nd International Conference on Contemporary Education, Social Sciences and Humanities (ICCESSH 2017)* (pp. 1078–1080). Atlantis Press.

34. Khanna, *The Future is Asian,* p37. See also Lewis, M. E. (2012). *China's Cosmopolitan Empire: The Tang Dynasty.* Harvard University Press.

35. Karrar, H. H. (2012). From Pastoral Nomadism to Shuttle Trading: A Long View of Commerce and Modernity Along the Sino-Central Asian Border. Material Culture, Language and Religion in Central and Inner Asia; Toronto Studies in Central and Inner Asia, No. 10, p 202

36. Kalra, *The Silk Road*, p. 9.

37. Khanna, *The Future is Asian*, p. 39.

38. Adshead, S. A. M. (1993). *Central Asia in world history*. Palgrave Macmillan, p.5 .

39. Kalra, *The Silk Road*, p. 1.

40. Ibid, p. 94.

41. Abu-Lughod, *Before European hegemony*, p. 182.

42. Ibid, p. 154.

43. Kalra, *The Silk Road*.

44. Ibid, p. 24.

45. Dardess, J. (1972). From Mongol Empire to Yüan Dynasty: Changing Forms of Imperial Rule in Mongolia and Central Asia. *Monumenta Serica, 30*, 117–165, p. 117.

46. Kalra, *The Silk Road*, p. 24

47. Adshead, *Central Asia in World History*, p. 66.

48. Abu-Lughod, *Before European hegemony*, p. 156.

49. Kalra, *The Silk Road*, p. 5.

50. Khanna, *The Future is Asian*, p. 40.

51. "Mughal" is the Persian translation of "Mongol."

52. Khanna, *The Future is Asian*, p. 41.

53. Cummings, *Understanding Central Asia*, p. 35.

54. Liu, *The Silk Road in world history*, p. 110.

55. Khanna, *The Future is Asian*, p. 48–9.

56. Karrar, From Pastoral Nomadism to Shuttle Trading, p. 203.

Chapter 2

ASIA DIVIDED

China and Central
Asia During the Soviet Era

Modern-day Central Asia and the western parts of Xinjiang once constituted an approximate region known as "Turkestan," a term used by medieval Islamic writers, and later also used by the Tsarist Russians in the nineteenth century.[1] The term referred not to a nation state but simply to a region inhabited by Turkic peoples (though Turkestan was also inhabited by some non-Turkic peoples such as the Tajiks).[2] For most of history, despite the fact that the region was frequently under the control of foreign powers, it was always somewhat fluid in terms of trade and the movement of people, and local cultures were never greatly disrupted by foreign rule.[3] The Sino-Russian border, established in the eighteenth and nineteenth centuries by the imperial Chinese and Russian powers, was the first rigid division to be created across Turkestan. It was drawn mostly along natural barriers and with little regard for the peoples it divided, such as Kazakhs, Kyrgyz, Uyghurs, Dungans and Pamiri Tajiks.

Further divisions within Turkestan were created following the establishment of the Soviet Union. The Central Asian region was split into five Soviet Socialist Republics (SSRs): the Uzbek and Turkmen SSRs were established in 1924, the Tajik SSR in 1929, and the Kazakh and Kyrgyz SSRs in 1936. The region was incorporated into a unified structure under which the politics and economics of the republics were monitored by Moscow. From this point until the collapse of the USSR in 1991, Central Asia's relationship with China fell into the broader category of Sino-Soviet relations.

BAZAAR TRADE IN CENTRAL ASIA

Physical markets, known as bazaars, have been a major feature of Central Asian society for centuries, reaching back to the ancient Silk Roads trade. Trade and pastoral nomadism were the two main vocations of steppe inhabitants for thousands of years. However, Central Asia's incorporation into the Russian Empire and subsequently the Soviet Union changed this. Both of these powers perceived such vocations as pre-modern economic activities. Central Asia came to be seen as a "backwater where forces of production were at lower levels of development."[4] Under the Soviet Union, trade was further condemned within state discourse as immoral, as it was perceived to constitute individualistic profiteering. Soviet economic values "privileged industrial and agricultural production as the true core of economic activity,"[5] and markets selling consumer goods were seen as disordered and uncivilised.[6] Large-scale land cultivation schemes as part of the Soviet Union's "modernisation" drive took Central Asians away from their traditional vocations.[7]

Nonetheless, bazaars persisted, though with important modifications, throughout the Soviet era, despite legal restrictions on trade and the fact that the state cast trade as an immoral activity. Legal private entrepreneurship in the Soviet Union was officially limited to selling surplus agricultural produce and locally-produced artisanal crafts in *kolkhoz* (collective farm) markets. Trading anything else, such as foreign consumer goods, was illegal. In practice, however, trade laws were not always enforced by local officials.[8] *Kolkhoz* markets were used to sell goods smuggled from abroad and stolen goods from state enterprises. There was, therefore, by no means a total repression of private trade in the Soviet Union. Furthermore, state policy towards private enterprise in the Soviet era did not remain static over time: it went in cycles of tighter and looser regulation. There were several periods in which the state established maximal control over production and distribution: these resulted in the growth of black-market trade and subsequent economic downturn. The state then responded to this by allowing limited forms of enterprise back into the legal economy.[9]

THE EARLY YEARS OF
THE SINO-SOVIET RELATIONSHIP

The relationship between the Soviet Union and the People's Republic of China over the second half of the twentieth century was central in determining patterns of trade, both formal and informal, between Central Asia and China. The 1917 Bolshevik Revolution in Russia inspired the formation of the Communist Party of China (CPC) nearly four years later. The People's Republic of China was formally inaugurated on October 1, 1949 and the CPC became the sole government party of China from then on. Prior to this, China had been engaged in a decade of intense warfare due to its involvement in the Second World War and the three years of Civil War that followed. As a result, the newly-established state desperately needed to industrialize. This meant that the promise of foreign assistance from the Soviet Union, who were industrially experienced and had backed the CPC during the Civil War, was very much welcomed. From the Soviet Union's perspective, China was the first major Asian nation to fall under communist rule and to adopt communist methods to promote economic development. They hoped that if China could achieve rapid economic development, this would constitute strong evidence for the superiority of the communist system and would influence the rest of Asia.[10]

In 1950, within the context of the early Cold War years and a hostile and defensive United States, the two states signed a Treaty of Friendship, Alliance and Mutual Assistance. Support from the Soviet Union played a prominent role in China's industrialisation. In the 1950s, the Soviet Union supplied China with loans amounting to roughly 6.87 billion Soviet Rubles ($1.7bn) of which around 6.29 billion went to military aid, and the rest to industrialisation. Most of those loans were repaid by Chinese export of trade items.[11] The Soviet Union supported China with industrial projects in mining, electricity, metals, chemistry, aerospace and defence. The number of Soviet-aided industrial projects was 50 in 1950, 141 in 1953 and by 1959 had increased to around 250. In many cases, the Soviet Union supplied all of the machinery, directed its installation, and left only when production had begun. According to Zhou Enlai, the Chinese Prime Minister and Foreign Minister, during 1949 and 1959 the USSR supplied 10,800 technicians, in addition to whom 1,500 came from the Soviet satellite states in Central Europe. Between 1951 and 1957, the Soviets claimed to have trained 13,600 Chinese students, workers and specialists in the USSR.[12]

In the 1950s, the Soviet Union and the PRC were principal trade partners to each other. The value of USSR-PRC trade grew from $238.4m in 1950 to peak at $2.1bn in 1959.[13] Most of the trade goods were exchanged based on annual formal negotiations and bilateral trade protocol. Instead of paying goods in fiat currency, both sides tracked item-to-item transactions by maintaining an official ledger which was cleared annually. The state-owned corporations in charge of foreign trade on each side bartered commodities item by item with their counterparts. The price of the trade items was denominated in Soviet Rubles up until 1970 (when the two sides agreed to change the currency to Swiss Francs).[14] China's imports from the Soviet Union were mostly means of production for its industrialisation, such as various types of machinery and equipment. In 1959, for example, machinery accounted for 62.6% of China's imports from the Soviet Union. China's exports to these countries consisted largely of raw materials and agricultural products, as well as native produce of which cereals, edible oils and foodstuffs made up the largest portion. This satisfied the domestic needs of the

USSR, whose imbalanced economic structure stressed the development of heavy industry.[15] China also provided the USSR with strategic materials such as non-ferrous metals and rare metals, which were extremely valuable to its development of weapons and technology. From 1950 to 1962, the Chinese province of Xinjiang provided the USSR with 100 thousand tons of lithium concentrate, which is used in the development of thermonuclear weapons.[16]

THE DETERIORATION OF SINO-SOVIET RELATIONS

The warm relationship between the two Communist allies came to an end in the 1960s with the so-called "Sino-Soviet split." When Nikita Khrushchev succeeded Joseph Stalin as the General Secretary of the Soviet Communist Party, he delivered a famous speech condemning Stalin's legacy. Alongside this, he also announced a strategy of peaceful coexistence with the United States, adopting a more lenient foreign policy towards capitalism. Both of these positions were problematic for the PRC: Mao disagreed with the public condemnation of Stalin, and the USSR's new foreign policy stood in contrast with China's support for Lenin's belief in the inevitability of the war between capitalism and communism. These ideological differences, along with a dispute over the PRC's approach towards domestic economic development and its relationship with India and Taiwan, caused a rupture in political relations between China and the Soviet Union. Both sides made attempts to fix the alliance, but ultimately these failed.[17] In 1960, the Soviet leaders tore up the agreements on technical assistance to China, and recalled all Soviet experts working there.[18] The value of Sino-Soviet trade followed a downward trajectory during the 1960s: from being worth $8.27bn in 1961, it fell to $47m in 1970.[19] Sino-Soviet trade as a proportion of China's total trade fell from 48% in 1959 to 1% in 1971.[20]

The Sino-Soviet split also had an impact on the movement of people between China and the Soviet Union. Up until the 1960s, large ethnic migrations between China and Central Asia had been a common feature of the region, meaning that Turkestan maintained its cultural and linguistic unity.[21] Hundreds of thousands moved from Xinjiang into Central Asia from the 1870s up until the early 1960s. These migrations sustained the ethnic connections between Xinjiang and Central Asia. In the 1960s, however, the Sino-Soviet border was closed, bringing an end to major migrations.

   With the deterioration of political relations between the two states emerged border disputes. In the nineteenth century, the Tsarist government had signed twenty-four border treaties acquiring vast territories from Qing China[22] as well as other agreements granting the Russian empire spheres of influence and extra-territorial rights in China. During the Soviet era, these territories consisted of two sections of the Sino-Soviet frontier: one part between the Chinese province of Xinjiang and the Soviet Central Asian republics, and the other between the Heilongjiang province (Manchuria) and north-eastern Siberia. Although in 1924 the Soviet Union denounced all Russian spheres of influence, extra-territorial rights and consular jurisdiction in China, the borders between the two states remained undefined.[23]

   In 1963, China publicly proposed the possibility of revision of the frontiers for the first time. The Communist Party's official news-paper, the People's Daily, mentioned nine treaties that Qing China had been forced to sign. The Soviet Government responded by issu-ing a statement that the Chinese had "systematically violated" the Soviet border. Tensions on the China-Soviet border subsequently accelerated. According to Chinese sources, in 1962 Soviet agencies and personnel had carried out "large scale subversive activities in the Ili region of Xinjiang and incited several tens of thousands of [Chinese] citizens into going to the Soviet Union."[24] In contrast, the reports from Moscow stated that riots occurred in Xinjiang among the Muslim Kazakhs, Uighurs and other nationalities, with the consequence that between the middle of 1962 and September 1963 about 50,000 fled from Xinjiang into the USSR. Boundary nego-tiations began in Beijing in February 1964, but were suspended in

May that same year without any progress achieved.[25] Armed clashes between Soviet and Chinese frontier guards also occurred years later in March 1969 in a small uninhabited island, known to the Russians as Damansky Island and to the Chinese as Zhenbao Island, which marked the lowest level of Sino-USSR relations.[26]

In the 1970s, the Chinese government made substantial adjustments to its foreign policy. It shifted from advocating world revolution—"down with imperialists, revisionists and reactionaries (*dadao dixiufan*)"—to a more pragmatic policy of "alliance with the United States to deter the Soviet Union (*lianMei kangSu*)" as a strategic counterweight to the perceived Soviet threat.[27] Nixon made his famous diplomatic visit to China in 1972, and the Sino-US rift began to ease internationally: as China emerged from the Cultural Revolution, its relationship with the non-socialist world slowly improved, and it was admitted to the United Nations in 1971.

To prevent the United States from gaining an advantage from the Sino-Soviet dispute, Soviet relations with China in the 1970s showed signs of revival, marked by substantial growth in trade and renewed restoration of border talks. A new trade agreement was concluded in 1970 after having been suspended since 1967.[28] The value of Sino-Soviet trade in 1971 recovered to $149m, about three times that in 1970.[29] In spite of the gradual revival, however, trade still remained at a low level in the 1970s. The value of Sino-Soviet trade only accounted for 1-4% of the total volume of Chinese foreign trade and 0.2-0.8% of the Soviet trade in the 1970s. The pattern of trade remained consistent, with the Soviet Union supplying machinery and equipment for China's raw materials and consumer goods.[30] From October 1969 to April 1978, the border negotiations between the two states continued, though still with little progress being made. Following the heightening intensity of Vietnamese military actions against Cambodia, the Soviet Union took Vietnam's side whilst China took Cambodia's. In 1979, the Soviet Union sent its troops and assistance to Afghanistan in an attempt to support the newly-established pro-Soviet regime, which aroused concerns in China regarding security at its south-western border. As a result of these developments, the late 1970s saw the rise of tension between China and the Soviet Union.[31] In 1979, when the 1950 treaty of friendship, alliance and mutual assistance between two states faced expiration next year, the Chinese government announced that it would not extend the treaty, but it offered to negotiate with the USSR on the improvement of bilateral relations.[32]

THE BEGINNINGS OF RENEWED COOPERATION

The 1980s witnessed a revival of Sino-Soviet relations. In 1982, Soviet General Secretary Leonid Brezhnev made a speech in Tashkent, the capital of the Uzbek SSR, in which he stressed that Moscow was prepared to enter into negotiations to improve relations with China without preconditions. Five rounds of talks were held between October 1982 and November 1984 on the normalization of Sino-Soviet relations. In 1985, the Chinese Vice Premier Yao Yilin visited Moscow, where both sides agreed to deepen their relationships. A five-year agreement (1986–1990) was signed to replace the annual one, and an agreement to strengthen educational and technical ties was also signed. The Chinese leaders insisted that cooperative Sino-Soviet relations would come only with the resolution of three obstacles: "Soviet military presence on China's north border, Soviet occupation of Afghanistan, and the most serious one, Soviet support for Vietnam's occupation of Cambodia."[33]

In 1985, Mikhail Gorbachev came to power in the Soviet Union and prioritised the strengthening of Moscow-Beijing relations. In October of that year, Chinese leader Deng Xiaoping proposed that "if the Soviet Union and China are able to reach an understanding and succeed in urging Vietnam to withdraw its troops from Cambodia, I am willing to meet Gorbachev." In May 1988, the Vietnamese Communist Party Politburo issued a plan providing for withdrawal of Vietnamese forces by the end of 1990 as part of an effort to improve its relations with both China and the United States.

Gorbachev finally visited China for four days in 1989, signalling the end of two decades of Sino-Soviet hostility.[34]

The 1980s also saw significant changes in trade patterns. Until the late 1970s, China's foreign trade had been heavily controlled by the central government. However, Mao Zedong's death in 1976 was followed two years later by the appointment as leader of Deng Xiaoping, who began to introduce major foreign trade reforms. China reduced the number of controlled trade items in its national trade plan: before the reforms, the trade of about 3,000 items was controlled by the government, but by the end of 1986, the number of controlled export items was down to only 38. China also began to decentralise its foreign trade to regional governments and enterprises. During the 1980s, the Soviet Union likewise relaxed its regulations on foreign trade. As a result of the decentralisation of foreign trade rights in both states, private enterprises and regional administrations started to establish themselves in Sino-Soviet trade.

In 1982, the Ministry of Foreign Trade of China and the Soviet Ministry of Foreign Trade formally agreed to resume border trade in Heilongjiang and Inner Mongolia, which had plummeted since the Sino-Soviet split. In the north-eastern Heilongjiang province, 30 cities and 188 enterprises were allowed to directly trade with Soviet counterparts. China also began border trade with the Soviet Union in the western provinces of Jilin and Xinjiang, in 1986 and 1987 respectively.[35] The Chinese state facilitated border trade with Kyrgyzstan and Kazakhstan by establishing border markets and checkpoints in Xinjiang.[36] The first border checkpoint was built in 1986 at Khorgas, a Chinese town on the Xinjiang–Kazakhstan border connecting northern Xinjiang to Almaty, the Kazakh capital at the time. The economic success of Khorgas prompted Chinese authorities to open additional border markets in Xinjiang.

Border trade was conducted over and above the bilateral barter trade agreement. The regional administrations and firms involved in border trade were encouraged to seek business opportunities and to be responsible for their own profits and losses. The value of border trade grew rapidly, even faster than the inter-government barter trade, thus reducing the latter's monopoly. The value of border trade from 1983-7 in Heilongjiang reached 139 billion Swiss francs (the value from 1957 to 1967 was about 54.9 million Swiss francs). The total volume of Sino-Soviet border trade climbed to 159 million Swiss francs in 1987, more than seven times that in 1983.[37]

As well as formal border trade, informal trade also grew rapidly between the two states. Ethnic minorities became particularly involved in this: for example, Soviet and Chinese Uyghurs were able to visit family members and at the same time to establish a cross-border shuttle trade.[38] However, the boom in informal trade brought reputational problems for China. It attracted a large number of shuttle traders rushing to sell Chinese products to Central Asia, some of whom sold counterfeits products into Central Asian markets in order to maximise their profits. Consumers were disappointed by the poor quality, and critical reports began to appear in the local media. Nonetheless, the emerging border trade of the late 1980s marked the beginnings of a huge growth in trade as an occupation: trade would soon become—once again—a major source of livelihoods in Central Asia.

CONCLUSION

The four decades from the establishment of the Sino-Soviet alliance in 1950 to the collapse of the Soviet Union in 1991 witnessed complex transformations in the Sino-Soviet relationship. In the 1950s, the newly-established Chinese communist state and the Soviet Union were strategic allies, with the Soviet Union playing a significant role in China's industrialization. However, their close relationship deteriorated in the 1960s due to different ideologies, border issues and disputes over Sino-Indian and -Taiwanese relations. The relationship between the two states was not officially normalized until the 1980s.

If we take a long historical perspective on the region known as Turkestan, it becomes evident that the fragmentation of this region into two centralising states was an anomaly. The border between Xinjiang and Central Asia was largely artificial and divided numerous ethnic groups. During the Sino-Soviet split, the movement of people and goods was restricted to an extent never seen before. As a result, the collapse of the Soviet Union and the opening up of borders produced great uncertainty. This fragmentation is gradually being undone, but many obstacles remain.

When we consider the legacy of four decades of Sino-Soviet relations in Central Asia, several points stand out. The polemics against China during the Soviet era have largely shaped the current perception of China in the post-Soviet space. As Catherine Owen discusses, Sinophobic discourses in Kyrgyzstan and Tajikistan tend to exaggerate China's "territorial acquisitions" due to Soviet propaganda during the border conflict.[39] This feeds into a widespread fear of Chinese expansionism. Furthermore, the perception that Chinese products are of bad quality has persisted to the present day.[40]

However, some Soviet legacies laid the groundwork for future cooperation. Firstly, the Chinese state's investment in infrastructure during the 1980s allowed informal trade to flourish across China's Western border. After the collapse of the Soviet Union in 1991, China continued to implement infrastructural changes to facilitate trade with the Central Asian countries, and it actively promoted informal border trade in order to encourage economic prosperity in Xinjiang. This meant that an increasing proportion of imported goods coming into Central Asia were from China. Secondly, when the Soviet Union collapsed in 1991, the dispute over the location of the frontier between Xinjiang and the Soviet Central Asian republics remained unresolved. This was initially the most highly prioritised issue for the newly independent Central Asian republics and China, and it shaped the subsequent relationship between them in important ways.

NOTES

1. Millward, J. A. (2007). *Eurasian crossroads: a history of Xinjiang*. *New York*: Columbia University Press, p. xi.
2. Turkic languages and peoples are also dispersed far beyond this region, across Siberia, the Middle East and Eastern Europe.
3. Raczka, W. (1998). Xinjiang and its Central Asian borderlands. Central Asian Survey, 17(3), 373–407.
4. Karrar, H. (2012). From Pastoral Nomadism to Shuttle Trading: A Long View of Commerce and Modernity Along the Sino-Central Asian Border. In Gervers, M. & Long, G. (Eds). *Material Culture, Language and Religion of Central and Inner Asia*. Asian Institute, University of Toronto, p.2 04.
5. Liu, M. (2012). *Under Solomon's throne: Uzbek visions of renewal in Osh*. Pittsburgh: University of Pittsburgh Press, p. 33.
6. Alff, H. (2015). Profiteers or Moral Entrepreneurs? Bazaars, Traders and Development Discourses in Almaty, Kazakhstan. International Development Planning Review, 37(3), 249–267, p. 256.
7. Karrar, From Pastoral Nomadism to Shuttle Trading, p. 204.
8. Hessler, J. (1998). A Postwar Perestroika? Toward a History of Private Enterprise in the USSR. Slavic Review, 57(3), 516–542.
9. Ibid, pp. 529–532.
10. Central Intelligence Agency of United States (CIA). (1959). Economic Relations of Communist China with the USSR since 1950 (Report No. 75). Central Intelligence Agency of United States: https://www.cia.gov/library/readingroom/docs/DOC_0000313442.pdf
11. Shen, Z. (2002). Guanyu 20 shiji 50 niandai sulian yuanhua daikuan de lishi kaocha [An Analysis of Soviet Economic Loans to China]. Zhongguo Jingjishi Yanjiu, 16(3), 83–93.
12. Jones, P., Kevill, S., & Day, A. J. (Eds.). (1985). *China and the Soviet Union 1949-84*. Harlow: Longman, p. 16.
13. Lu, N. (1990). Xinshiqi zhongsu jingji guanxi fazhan qianjing [Sino-Soviet Trade in 1980s]. Social Science Front, 6(20), 26–34. Retrieved from http://www.cqvip.com/qk/82161x/199002/1002872250.html
14. The shift in trading currency from Soviet Rubles to Swiss Francs resulted from the deterioration in relations between the two sides.
15. Zhang, P., & Huenemann, R. W. (1987). *China's Foreign Trade*. Oolichan: Lantzville, p. 113.
16. Jing, Z. (2016, November 30). Keketuohai sanhao kuangkeng de qianshijinsheng [the history of Koktokay No. 3 pegmatite]. China

Geological Survey. Retrieved from http://www.zgkyb.com/observa
tion/20161130_36752 .htm
17. Lüthi, L. M. (2010). The Sino-Soviet split: Cold War in the communist world (Vol. 124). Princeton University Press, pp. 46–48.
18. Yang, K. (2000). *The Sino-Soviet Border Clash of 1969: From
Zhenbao Island to Sino-American Rapprochement.* Cold War History, 1(1),
21–52.
19. *Chinese Foreign Trade Compilation Commission.* (1984). Beijing: Foreign Trade Press, p. 889. Cited from Lu, N. (1990). Xinshiqi
zhongsu jingji guanxi fazhan qianjing [Sino-Soviet Trade in 1980s].
Social Science Front, 6(20), 26–34. Retrieved from http://www.cqvip.com/
qk/82161x/199002/1002872250.html
20. Central Intelligence Agency of United States (CIA). (1972). *The
Revival of Sino-Soviet Trade* (Report No. 86). Central Intelligence Agency
of United States: https://www.cia.gov/library/readingroom/docs/CIA-RDP
85T00875R001700040019-6.pdf
21. Raczka, W. (1998). Xinjiang and its Central Asian borderlands.
Central Asian Survey, 17(3), 373–407.
22. Ma, X. (2001). *Shu li zhongsubianjie bianqianshi [An overview of
the history of Sino-Soviet border].* World Affairs, (11), 40–41. Retrieved
from http://mall.cnki.net/magazine/magadetail/SJZS200111.htm
23. Jones et al, *China and the Soviet Union*, pp. 87—88.
24. Li, D. (1999). Yita Incident in Xinjiang. [A Historical Investigation
into the 1962 Yita Incident in Xinjiang]. Dangshi Yanjiu Ziliao, 1–8. (4–5).
Retrieved from http://mjlsh.usc.cuhk.edu.hk/Book.aspx?cid=4&tid=4765
25. Jones, P., Kevill, S., & Day, A. J., pp. 89—90.
26. Gerson, M. S. (2010). The Sino-Soviet border conflict: Deterrence,
escalation, and the threat of nuclear war in 1969 (CRM D0022974.A2).
CNA. Retrieved from https://www.cna.org/CNA_files/PDF/D0022974.
A2.pdf
27. Jones, P., Kevill, S., & Day, A. J., p. 97.
28. Central Intelligence Agency of United States. (1972). The Revival
of Sino-Soviet Trade. Retrieved from https://www.cia.gov/library/reading-
room/docs/CIA-RDP85T00875R001700040019-6.pdf
29. *Chinese Foreign Trade Compilation Commission.* (1984). Beijing: Foreign Trade Press, p. 889. Cited from Lu, N. (1990). Xinshiqi
zhongsu jingji guanxi fazhan qianjing [Sino-Soviet Trade in 1980s].
Social Science Front, 6(20), 26–34. Retrieved from http://www.cqvip.com/
qk/82161x/199002/1002872250.html
30. Jones, P., Kevill, S., & Day, A. J., p. 117.

31. Garver, J. W. (1989). The" New Type" of Sino-Soviet Relations. Asian Survey, 29(12), 1136–1152.

32. Jones, P., Kevill, S., & Day, A. J., p. 138.

33. Ibid.

34. Ibid.

35. Liu, J. (1988). Zhongsu bianjing maoyi riquhuoyue [Sino-USSR border trade is getting more active]. Intertrade.(11), 6. 2

36. Karrar, H. (2013). Merchants, markets and the state: informality, transnationality and spatial imaginaries in the revival of Central Eurasian trade. Critical Asian Studies, 45, 459–80.

37. Liu, X. (1989). Zhonguo dongbei diqu tong sulian bianjing maoyi de xianzhuang fenxi [The Border Trade with the Soviet Union in Northeast China &. Russian]. East European & Central Asian Studies, 9(4), 75–80. Retrieved from China National Knowledge Infrastructure: http://www.cnki.net

38. Laruelle, M. & Peyrouse, S. (2012). *The Chinese Question in Central Asia: Domestic Order, Social Change, and the Chinese Factor.* London: Hurst, p. 98.

39. Owen, C. (2017). "The Sleeping Dragon Is Gathering Strength": Causes of Sinophobia in Central Asia. China Quarterly of International Strategic Studies, 3(01), 101–119.

40. Peyrouse, S. (2016). Discussing China: Sinophilia and Sinophobia in Central Asia. Journal of Eurasian Studies, 7(1), 14–23.

Chapter 3

FIVE INDEPENDENT STATES

1991-2013

As a result of the disintegration of the Soviet Union, five new countries emerged in the middle of the Asian continent: Kazakhstan, Kyrgyzstan, Tajikistan, Turkmenistan and Uzbekistan, all of which were former Soviet Socialist Republics. The five states began to embark on a process of state-building and market reforms; a process which varied widely between the states due to major differences in domestic conditions and in economic and foreign policy. This chapter looks at the new modes of both formal and informal cooperation that emerged between China and the Central Asian states during the first twenty years of their independence. These laid the groundwork for, and in many cases pre-empted, economic cooperation under the Belt and Road Initiative (BRI).

THE BORDER DELIMITATION AND THE UYGHUR DIASPORA

After the collapse of the Soviet Union, Beijing was prepared to conduct cautious but friendly diplomacy with the former Soviet republics. On September 7, 1991, the day after the USSR's collapse,

Qian Qichen, Chinese State Councillor and Foreign Minister, called the five foreign ministers of independent states in Central Asia and declared that the People's Republic of China government recognised their independence.[1] These five states likewise sought good diplomatic relations with China as they hoped to diversify their economic relationships outside of the Soviet bloc.[2]

The border issue was the most immediate problem that China and the new Central Asian states needed to solve. It was rooted in the historical relationship between China and Russia. With the 19th century decline of the Qing dynasty and the rise of the Russian empire, St Petersburg joined the foreign powers requesting territorial concessions from China. The Qing dynasty signed several treaties with the Russian empire, delimiting the frontier in North East Siberia and in Xinjiang.

The Treaty of Beijing (1860) gave the Tsarist empire commercial, diplomatic and territorial advantages. On its western border, China ceded to Russia the area including Semirechie (the area east of Lake Balkhash and south of the Zaysan lake), the lower Ili Valley and most of today's Kyrgyzstan. In subsequent years the Russians moved the border still further east, occupying the upper Ili district in Xinjiang. With the Treaty of St. Petersburg in 1881, the Chinese recovered the Ili, but Russia still controlled large areas to which Beijing laid claim.[3] The treaty created a no-man's land that spread across much of the Pamir Mountains.

These treaties were later perceived by Beijing to be unequal ones favouring the Russians. China raised the border issue in the 1960s, but because of poor relations between the two states after the Sino-Soviet split, the issue did not get resolved and the region remained under the control of the Soviet Union. This meant that when the Soviet Union collapsed and the five Central Asian states gained their independence, the question of the western part of the Sino-Soviet border was still unresolved. Tajikistan, Kazakhstan, and Kyrgyzstan all shared borders with China. Multilateral meetings were held involving these three countries and China in order to negotiate the territorial dispute. Russia was also involved so that the new Central Asian states would not be left alone and in a weak negotiating position.[4]

Kazakhstan and Kyrgyzstan had both resolved their border disputes with China by the end of the 1990s, though the Pamir Mountains remained a source of contention for Tajikistan and the dispute over this area was not resolved until 2002. China made significant compromises in the border dispute, conceding the majority of the territory that it had initially requested to the Central Asian countries. Given China's power, it could have threatened the survival of the young Central Asian states by removing large portions of their territory, but it did not.[5] The peaceful solution of the border disputes shows good will from both sides in the early years of interaction between Beijing and the young Central Asian states. This laid a solid foundation for their future cooperation in broader areas.

A second area on which China and the Central Asian countries cooperated was the Uyghur diaspora. As discussed in chapter 2, Xinjiang and its Central Asian neighbours have a similar ethnic composition and a shared culture. For example, over one million Kazakhs live in China's Xinjiang, and around 300,000 Uyghurs live in the five Central Asian states in total.[6] Uyghurs have long claimed Xinjiang as their ancestral land, whilst the Chinese state claims that since the first century AD, Xinjiang has been part of China. In fact, the history of the region known today as Xinjiang is much more complex than this: as discussed in chapter 1, it was incorporated into many different empires throughout history. Xinjiang was first conquered by the Chinese state during the Qing dynasty in the mid-eighteenth century, though the central government did not establish direct rule over the area until 1884. Following the founding of the Republic of China in 1911, central state control over Xinjiang was weak, and in the 1930s and 1940s, Uyghur nationalists established two short-lived "Eastern Turkestan Republics," though both of these states covered only a small proportion of Xinjiang.[7] From 1949 onwards, the People's Republic of China administered the region as the "Xinjiang Uyghur Autonomous Region," and central government control over the region has been strong ever since.

Uyghur nationalism had therefore been present to some degree within Xinjiang for much of the twentieth century. With the collapse of the Soviet Union, however, pro-independence Uyghur unrest gained international attention to a degree that it never had before. James Millward suggests that the reasons for this are complex. The raised profile of separatist activities may have been due to an actual increase in them, due to factors such as the independence of the Central Asian states, increased travel to and from Central Asia and rapid Han in-migration to Xinjiang. However, Millward points out that from the 1980s onwards, foreign journalists had much greater access to Xinjiang, and that the rise of the internet enabled both journalists and Uyghurs to disseminate information.

The independence of the Central Asian states gave China cause to collaborate with them on the Uyghur issue. Beijing expressed concern with "the spill-over effect of the resurgent terrorist activities in Central Asia on Xinjiang and its Uighur ethnic group":[8] for example, they were worried about the potential influence of the Taliban in Afghanistan. Beijing repeatedly sought assurance from its new neighbours that they would not support any ethno-separatist activities: this was an issue that it perceived could impact stability in Northwest China, as well as in the whole Central Asian region.[9]

The Central Asian states agreed to discourage independent Uyghur statehood, in return for economic and security cooperation with China. In the late 1990s, the Kazakh and Kyrgyz governments curtailed all Uyghur political activities and organizations. Since then, only Uyghur "cultural associations" have been allowed to operate.[10]

THE SHANGHAI COOPERATION ORGANIZATION: AN INSTITUTIONAL REGIONAL FRAMEWORK

During the border negotiation process, the Shanghai Group was created in 1996 for China, Russia, Kazakhstan, Kyrgyzstan and Tajikistan to negotiate the border issues and progressively demilitarize the borders in the region. As negotiations on border delimitation progressed, there was a spread of perceived threats brought by the Islamic fundamentalist movement across the Tajik and Kyrgyz border. In the Shanghai Group summits of 1999 and 2000, the heads of states agreed to address prevention of military threats and to consider actions to protect borders and combat terrorism. In 2001, Uzbekistan—a Central Asian state without a common border with China—joined the group, and the six states together signed the Declaration on the Establishment of the Shanghai Cooperation Organization (SCO). The Shanghai Five therefore transformed from a temporary dialogue mechanism into a permanent formal regional organization.[11] In 2006, Afghanistan, Mongolia, India, Pakistan and Iran were included in the SCO as "observer" countries. A decade later, in 2017, India and Pakistan became full members of the SCO. While the cross-border security concerns provided the initial impetus for the formation of SCO, its agenda also covers regional economic cooperation, and cultural collaboration in the area. As argued by Saxena and Kalra, "the SCO is also focusing on economic and social integration of the region and has gone to great lengths to create confidence in its desire to promote prosperity and cooperation."[12]

The May 2003 summit in Moscow concluded the development of the SCO's institutional framework. The SCO has two permanent bodies: the Secretariat of the SCO and the Regional Anti-Terrorist Structure (RATS). The Secretariat began to function in 2004, with its headquarters in Beijing dedicated to daily affairs. The RATS, located in Tashkent, is especially for the exchange and collection of intelligence on suspected military terrorists and organizations in the SCO member states.[13]

However, non-permanent organs are at the core of decision-making and inter-governmental communication in the organisation. The supreme decision-making body of the SCO is the Council of Heads of State (HSC), which meets annually to agree on guidelines for all important matters and sign off on agreements, programs and the next annual agenda.[14]

The SCO Council of Heads of Government (HGC) also meets once a year to discuss the organization's multilateral cooperation strategy and priority areas, to resolve current economic and other cooperation issues, and to approve the organisation's annual budget. In addition to HSC and HGC meetings, there are also meetings at the level of heads of parliament, secretaries of Security Councils, and ministers of government departments, as well as joint working groups to discuss strategies in specific areas.

The centrality of non-permanent organs to the SCO is important to emphasise as, whilst the BRI is not a formal organization like the SCO, its institutional design follows a similar philosophy. Both the SCO and the BRI are loose and informal institutional frameworks which mainly function to enhance high-level communication and diplomacy, rather than western-inspired political integration based on a common legal framework, as is the case with the EU. Decisions are made by the SCO members based on consensus through dialogue, rather than by voting. Similarly to the BRI, the SCO has very limited ability to enforce collective actions amongst its member states, meaning that the member states have ceded little sovereignty to the organization and have their own right to decide whether and how they will implement the actions proposed in the meeting.

The Declaration on the Establishment of the Shanghai Cooperation Organization stated the objective of the organization as follows:

> *"strengthening mutual trust, friendship and good neighbourliness between the member states; encouraging effective cooperation between them in the political, trade, economic, scientific, technical, cultural, educational, energy, transport, environmental and other fields; making joint efforts to maintain and ensure peace, security and stability in the region and establishing new, democratic, just and rational international political and economic order."*[15]

These objectives are, again, very similar to those espoused by Beijing for the BRI.

The members of the SCO place particular emphasis on security, aiming jointly to prevent the so-called "three evils" of Terrorism, Separatism and Extremism in the region. The SCO members have organized joint military exercises in border regions annually since

2003. The exercises signal the collective action of the SCO to combat non-traditional security threats in the region. However, they are also superficial to some extent: the participating troops of the exercise are mainly Russian, Chinese and Kazakh forces, and there is little real joint action across the armies during the exercises. Furthermore, the Central Asian states, especially Uzbekistan, have been avoiding large scale involvement based on their desire to maintain sovereignty.[16]

Although security concerns provided the initial impetus for the formation of the SCO, economic cooperation is also a major part of the SCO's agenda. In 2003, the SCO adopted the Program for Multilateral Trade and Economic Cooperation, setting out key objectives up until 2020, including the creation of favourable conditions across the region for the free movement of goods, capital, technology and services. In 2004, five working groups were established for electronics, commerce, customs, inspection of goods and harmonization of standards, and cooperation in investment. Although Beijing has eagerly proposed to make the SCO a free trade zone, Russia and the Central Asian states are less enthusiastic about the idea of a common market, fearing that their products cannot compete with Chinese goods.[17] Nonetheless, they very much welcome Chinese investment, cooperation on energy projects and the establishment of cross-regional transport corridors between China and Europe through Russia and Central Asia. Over 120 projects have been identified for action under the cooperation programme, although progress has been limited. The June 2006 summit established a number of economic structures, including the Moscow-based Business Council and the Interbank Association to prepare for a joint investment programme before 2010. The Business Council aims to foster direct contact between the institutions and businessmen of its member states, and contribute to the implementation of the SCO projects, while the Interbank Association "is a banking institution of six countries that at its own discretion determines feasibility of the projects based on the generally accepted banking standards."[18] The cooperation programme covers major infrastructure projects, transport, energy, telecommunications and cross-border trade. China has already funded some of those projects through financing or low-interest loans.

Some commentators portray the SCO as an antagonistic anti-western military alliance aiming to counter the US's presence in Central Asia. For example, Peter Brookes of the Heritage Foundation asserted that "Russia may be looking to create a 'new and improved' Asian Warsaw Pact, wielding large armies, big economies, nukes and lots of oil/gas."[19] The American political scientist Ariel Cohen warned that "the anti-American axis has already begun to work."[20] But such arguments may exaggerate the military side of the SCO. Rather than combatting an external security risk, as is usually the motivation for the formation of a military alliance, the organisation aims to reduce transnational crime and terrorism within and between the SCO member states.[21] Its security work is limited to soft action on anti-terrorism issues, and there is no collective SCO military force: indeed, the idea of creating such a force is excluded from the SCO's objectives. The SCO's focus is more on comprehensive objectives such as economic and social development agendas. In other words, the SCO is an organization for overall regional development, rather than a military alliance.

Other scholars argue that the SCO has made little progress in achieving functional cooperation, which has reduced its effectiveness in both making and enforcing collective decisions. As a result, for example, "the goal of trade and investment facilitation is far from being reached and a free trade area is still considered taboo."[22] Even in the relatively developed field of security cooperation, SCO solidarity was challenged when members could not reach an agreement on joint support for Russian military action against Georgia in 2008. In an even more humiliating episode, the organization could do little when Kyrgyzstan plunged into domestic turmoil in 2010. On the other hand, the SCO's use of decision-making based on consensus leaves enough space for the Central Asian republics to maintain their sovereignty. The flexible and multilateral approach is particularly important for these countries given that they face two major external powers.[23]

The SCO should be credited as a creative regional institution that formalizes negotiation among the member states, encouraging greater association with each other. The inclusion of Russia and China in the SCO helped to avoid the possible tension between the two major external powers over their influence in Central Asia, where Russia perceives it has "natural influence" after the collapse of the Soviet Union, but where China's economic influence has rapidly increased. The SCO is an effective attempt to encourage collective action on issues in the region, such as the border dispute, non-traditional security threats and economic cooperation agendas. When we look at the SCO's role in the evolution of relations between China and Central Asia, the creation of a stable institutional framework for cooperation between these states is a major achievement given the hostile attitudes they had towards each other for much of the Soviet era. The frequent dialogue and exchange at different levels under the SCO provides the Central Asian republics with important channels to better understand China and to build up confidence towards their neighbour.

The SCO marks an important step in China-Central Asia relations. Its multilateral approach helped China to engage more closely with issues in Central Asia, and enabled the Central Asian republics to strengthen their diplomacy with larger powers in the region. Although the achievement of the SCO in its specific agendas has been criticised as limited, it has nonetheless been successful in reinforcing trust in regional cooperation, bringing about "the gaining of knowledge about the other, person-to-person relations, and the forming of—at least partial—relations of confidence with China."[24] The regional economic cooperation under the SCO shows very similar characteristics to the future Belt and Road Initiative (BRI) projects with regards to the major financial inputs from China and the emphasis on infrastructure. In 2013, when China proposed the BRI, it included the SCO as one of the most important cooperation mechanisms. From 2014 onwards, the heads of governments of SCO members officially echoed their support for the BRI. Some of the programs initiated by the SCO in previous years were also brought under the umbrella of the BRI.

CHINESE ECONOMIC INROADS IN CENTRAL ASIA

Whilst China and the Central Asian republics were negotiating on the issues of Uyghur separatism and border delimitation, trade between China and Central Asia was increasing steadily. The infrastructural changes that the Chinese government had begun to implement in the late 1980s in order to facilitate trade continued into the 1990s. Further new border checkpoints were opened, such as the China-Kazakhstan border post at Dostyk-Alashankou, and in 1993 visa-free entry into China for Central Asians for up to three days was introduced.[25]

The period between 1992–1996 also witnessed the signing of multiple friendship treaties and agreements. The volume of trade exchanges between China and Central Asia at that time was relatively low, and much lower than Central Asia's trade with Russia, Turkey or even Iran. According to Chinese figures, the period from 1992 to 1996 witnessed an increase in the total volume of trade between China and Central Asian states from $459m to $778m, further increasing to $1.51bn in 2001.[26] After the establishment of the SCO in 2001, Sino-Central Asian trade boomed along with Chinese investment in Central Asian hydrocarbons and infrastructure. Before the world economic crisis in 2008, trade between China and Central Asia had already reached $30.8bn.[27] Despite the downturn in 2009, Sino-Central Asian trade continued to maintain a high volume and reached $50.8bn in 2014.[28] Importantly, though, all of these figures represent only the formal economy. The informal economy, to be discussed later in this chapter, also took off rapidly after the collapse of the Soviet Union.

80–90% of Chinese exported goods to Central Asia are finished, diversified goods, such as machinery, processed foodstuffs, textiles, shoes and electronic products. Conversely, over 85% of China's imports from Central Asia include raw materials, petrol, and ferrous and non-ferrous metals. The consumer products imported from China are popular in Central Asia because their low prices suit the relatively low living standards of the majority of Central Asians, whilst they are also capable of satisfying the growing consumer technology demands of the middle class. However, the rapid influx of cheap goods has also posed challenges: it has threatened the competitiveness of local producers, pushing economies away from activities with higher value-added and towards the export of raw materials.[29]

The poor transport infrastructure in Central Asia has hindered the region's ability to trade with China. Most of the transport systems in Central Asia are Soviet-era legacies whose refurbishment would have required a large financial input beyond the means of the young states. Of the eight border checkpoints between China and Central Asia, just four—Dostyk, Khorgos, Irkeshtam and Torugart—have been operational as regional trade hubs, while the others are only used by small scale traders or local people due to geographical isolation and the lack of transport infrastructure. Since the 1990s, the Central Asian republics have been seeking to improve their infrastructure system with the support of international actors. For example, in the mid-1990s, Uzbekistan proposed a railway project linking its highly populated Ferghana Valley with Kashgar in Xinjiang via Kyrgyzstan. However, the project is still on hold at the time of writing due to political tensions, divergences of opinion, and technical challenges.

One successful project has been the rehabilitation of the Osh-Sarytash-Irkeshtam road. A border checkpoint at Irkeshtam in southern Kyrgyzstan was opened in 1997. Situated 240km from Osh and 250km from Kashgar, the checkpoint is located on the most direct route between the Ferghana Valley and Xinjiang. However, because of the poor conditions of the road and the mountainous region through which the route passes, prior to the road rehabilitation it would have taken four hours on average to reach the town of Sarytash, which is around 70km away, and a whole day to get to Osh. In 2004, the

Development Bank of China, China's largest policy bank pledged a grant of RMB 60m for the refurbishment of the road.

The rehabilitation work on this 258km-long road from Osh to the China-Kyrgyzstan border was finished in 2012. This project was jointly financed by the Asian Development Bank, Islamic Development Bank, Export-Import (Exim) Bank of China and Development Bank of China. The contract was awarded to a leading Chinese state-owned enterprise, the China Road & Bridge Corporation. China funded 135km of the project in total, through combination of a loan from the Exim Bank of China and a scheme that allowed Kyrgyzstan to swap resources for investments whereby, in exchange for Chinese financing, the Kyrgyz government allowed the Chinese company Full Gold Mining to develop the gold deposit Ishtamberdy in Southern Kyrgyzstan.[30] The Osh-Sarytash-Irkeshtam road is part of the transportation corridor that links China, Kyrgyzstan, Tajikistan and Uzbekistan.

China has also funded electricity infrastructure in Central Asia. For example, in 2009, the Chinese company Tebian Electric Apparatus Stock Company (CTEAS) finished the construction work of a 500-kilovolts power transmission line in Tajikistan. The project aimed to bring electricity to rural villages in South Tajikistan by connecting northern and southern Tajik power grids. The contracting agreement was signed at the SCO Summit in 2006. The cost of the project was around $284m, $270m of which was provided as a loan from the Exim Bank of China.[31]

In the mobile telecommunications sector, the poor quality of the services on offer for landline telephones in Central Asia favoured a rapid expansion in mobile phone use. As a result, collective meetings between the national telecommunication firms in the SCO states took place under the SCO framework. Chinese telecommunications companies — mainly China Telecom, Huawei Technologies and ZTE (Shenzhen Zhongxing Telecom Equipment Corporation) — have been active in undertaking the modernization of telephone networks, installation of telecommunication stations with digital systems, supplying telecommunication equipment and the development of internet access.[32]

Chinese firms are characterized by their competitive price and technological know-how, which often gives them an advantage in contracting these projects. They have sometimes been criticised for bringing their own workers without creating sufficient jobs for locals, and for aggressive methods of competition backed by Beijing's diplomatic support. However, there is no doubt that generous investment in infrastructure is needed if the landlocked Central Asian states are to generate enough energy to build their industrial capacity, improve their connectivity with international markets, and move towards their historical role as transit hubs for goods travelling across Eurasia.

Apart from trade and infrastructure, China's economic presence in Central Asia is also characterised by its large-scale investments in hydrocarbons, which China sees as vital for its energy security. China transformed from an oil-exporting country to a net importer in 1993, and in 2017 it surpassed the United States as the largest importer in the world.[33] Since 1997, Beijing has aimed to increase and diversify its energy imports in order to address the increasing demand for petroleum and to prevent its oil supply from being affected by political hazards in the Middle East. Beijing thus turned to suppliers in Central Asia, mainly Kazakhstan, Turkmenistan, and Uzbekistan, which are the most significant hydrocarbon suppliers outside the Persian Gulf states. Geographical proximity also makes pipeline transportation possible, which is safer than using oil tankers passing through intermediate countries and across the sea.

The entry of Chinese players into the Central Asian hydrocarbon market was marked by an agreement reached in 1997 under which China's giant State-Owned Enterprise, the China National Petroleum Corporation (CNPC), and its subsidiaries were invited to invest in Kazakh oil fields. The CNPC acquired 60% of shares in Kazakhstan's fourth-largest oil company Aktobe Munay Gas, which has access to two oil and gas sites in Kazakhstan. After 2003, the CNPC and other Chinese companies completed a new wave of acquisitions of oil fields and petroleum firms in Kazakhstan, including the North Buzachi field, the Bars exploration site, Darkhan field (acquired jointly with the Kazakh firm KazMunayGas) and the firms PetroKazakhstan and KarazhanbasMunai. By 2010, China was already in charge of approximately a quarter of Kazakh oil production.[34] The Kazakhstan-China oil pipeline—China's first direct oil import pipeline—was also built in the early twenty-first century. The pipeline starts at Atasu on the shores of the Caspian Sea and ends at Dushanzi in Xinjiang, transporting the oil from several fields exploited by Chinese firms. Over a period of almost three years from 2006 to 2009, the pipeline transported up to 20.39 million tons of oil, making up twelve percent of the oil that China imports each year.[35] Although Chinese firms established themselves in Central Asian petroleum markets fairly quickly, the most promising oil sites were nonetheless already taken by western and Russian competitors who had established themselves as soon as the market opened up.

In contrast with the complexity of the oil market, China enjoyed rapid progress in the gas market in Turkmenistan. In 2006, the Turkmen president proposed the construction of a gas pipeline, and China and the Central Asian states reached an agreement to build a pipeline from Turkmenistan, via Uzbekistan and Kazakhstan, to Khorgos in Xinjiang. The pipeline starts at Gedaim on the border of Turkmenistan and Uzbekistan, running through central Uzbekistan and southern Kazakhstan, and reaches the border of China at Khorgos in Xinjiang. The first two initial pipelines were inaugurated in December 2009 and "line C" of the pipeline became operational in May, 2014. According to BP statistical Reviews of World Energy, China imported 36.2 billion cubic metres (bcm) of gas via pipeline in 2017 and 24.1bcm of gas in 2016. The pipeline also allowed Central Asian states to diversify their gas exports, which were highly dependent on Russian-controlled pipelines.[36]

TRADE OUTSIDE OF STATE REGULATION

Beyond formal cooperation, the period from the 1990s onwards has seen a huge increase in informal trade. Imported goods from neighbouring countries for sale at bazaars constitute the vast majority of this trade. The income contribution of bazaar trade to Central Asian countries is difficult to calculate since imports usually bypass formal regulatory mechanisms and therefore go unreported in the official country trade statistics.[37] However, Hasan Karrar estimates that the turnover for Kyrgyzstan's three largest bazaars is roughly 40% more than its formal GDP.[38]

The collapse of the Soviet Union brought a huge influx of the labour force into bazaar trade in the newly independent Central Asian states. Most people entered trade out of economic neces-sity, following the rapid decrease in public-sector salaries and the disintegration of state enterprises as they were cut off from Soviet era suppliers and customers.[39] In the case of Kyrgyzstan, from 1991 to 1996 the share of public sector employment in total employment decreased from 74% to 27.5%.[40] Many of those who took up trading as a means of survival were therefore from professional occupations, including former teachers, engineers and bureaucrats. Women in particular suffered from lack of employment and were more likely than men to become self-employed traders. It is estimated that by 2004, at least one in ten "economically active" Kyrgyz citizens were officially registered as working in the trade sector.[41] It was common that citizens from rural areas would migrate to cities in order to find work at bazaars.[42] The impact of bazaar trade on the standards of living of the Central Asian countries should not be underestimated: it "helped hundreds of thousands of Central Asian households—that is, millions of people—to survive the 1990s."[43] From the end of the Soviet period in 1989 to the year 2005, the number of bazaars in Kyrgyzstan quadrupled.[44]

The ways in which these goods are imported has changed over time. Shuttle traders were already operating illegally during the Soviet Union, and more so with the advent of *perestroika* (economic restructuring) which brought market-like reforms in the 1980s.[45] Much greater numbers of people took up shuttle trading with the breakup of the Soviet Union and the concurrent legalisation of trade. Throughout the 1990s, shuttle traders who had acquired suf-ficient capital set up direct trading relationships with manufacturers in China and placed large orders with them, as opposed to buying goods at Chinese malls.[46] In the second half of the 1990s, trade at the state level increased due to the establishment of official trading relations with China, which brought about a reduction in the volume of cross border trade. By the early 2000s, large-scale movement of cargo by shipping companies became more dominant, though shuttle trading has continued to happen to the present day.[47]

The physical form taken by bazaars has also changed in the years following independence. Some bazaars were continuations of Soviet-era farmers' markets, *kolkhozy*, whilst others started from scratch. Central Asia's largest bazaar, the Dordoi in Kyrgyzstan, began in 1992 with minimal infrastructure, with goods "sold from blankets on the ground or car bonnets."[48] By the late 1990s the bazaar administration had introduced shipping containers to be used for warehousing and sales. Dordoi has grown further since then: restaurants, mosques and currency exchange services have been established on its premises. As well as acquiring built structure, bazaars have been subjected to increasing legal regulations over time: traders today have to pay taxes and other dues to the bazaar administration. Bazaars are thus now well-established institutions. The growth of bazaar trade has also given rise to a large number of related service professions, such as logistics, translation services and commercial services.[49]

Of the Central Asian countries, Kyrgyzstan and Kazakhstan have pursued the most open trade policies since independence and there-fore are subject to the greatest quantities of transnational bazaar trade. Kyrgyzstan, initially the most dedicated of the Central Asian countries to Washington-Consensus economic reform,[50] has the most liberal cross-border regulations and has thus become a major re-exporter of bazaar goods. In Kyrgyzstan's two largest bazaars, the Dordoi in Bishkek and Kara-Suu in the South, a significant amount of wholesale trade takes place, as well as retailing to con-sumers. Similarly, the Kazakh government "actively encouraged international trade" in the decade following independence.[51] The opening up of Kyrgyzstan and Kazakhstan to trade coincided with an increase in export manufacturing hubs in countries such as China and Turkey during the 1990s,[52] which meant that large quantities of cheap consumer goods became readily available. In 2008, Kyrgyzstan and Kazakhstan together were estimated to have received over four fifths of China's total exports to Central Asia.[53] Goods entering Kyrgyzstan and Kazakhstan came to be predominantly from China due to the Chinese government's efforts to facilitate trade through building infrastructure as well as the availability of low-cost Chinese goods. The share of Chinese imports in total imports to Kyrgyzstan was estimated at ninety-three percent in 2007.[54]

Due to its role as a re-exporter, Kyrgyzstan is of particular importance for the entry of Chinese consumer goods into the rest of Central Asia and southern regions of Russia. From the 1990s onwards, it has become more profitable for traders in Kyrgyzstan's neighbouring countries to travel to Bishkek than to China to buy Chinese-made goods. After buying the goods in Bishkek's bazaars, the traders return to their home countries to sell them. Spector observes that bazaars in Kyrgyzstan have thus been fulfilling the demand of neighbouring countries as well as of the domestic population.[55] Kyrgyzstan has become a particularly successful re-exporter for a number of reasons. The accession of Kyrgyzstan and China to the World Trade Organisation in 1998 and 2001 respectively guaranteed low tariffs on Chinese imports for Kyrgyzstan.[56] It was also distinguished from other post-Soviet countries as its government adopted favourable policies towards bazaar trade, demanding "only limited fees and regulations for bazaar traders", whilst other governments in the region viewed bazaar trade negatively, seeing it as an activity outside of state regulations.[57]

A further facilitator of trade with China has been the close ethnic and religious commonalities between Kazakhstan, Kyrgyzstan and Xinjiang. Commercial networks based upon ethnic connections, which had begun to grow in the 1980s, continued to expand. Ethnic minorities in Central Asia who had maintained close familial connections with kin in Xinjiang became involved in the cross-border trade, either operating in the bazaars or in related businesses—for example, hiring out warehouses or providing accommodation for travelling merchants.[58]

However, different minorities have not been equally included in trade. The scholars Marlene Laruelle and Sebastien Peyrouse point out that throughout the 1990s and 2000s, Uyghurs became economically marginalised. This was firstly because once Sino-Central Asian trade was brought under state control, companies owned by the Han Chinese arrived in Xinjiang and outcompeted the Uyghurs due to their access to supplies from large production centres in south-east China. And secondly, the connection of some Uyghurs with separatism and Islamist activities has made them the subject of political suspicion, making it harder for them to participate in transnational trade networks.[59]

This has not been such a problem for the Dungans, who are not perceived as being associated with separatist activities.[60] The Dungans are a Muslim ethnic group descended from the Hui people of the Chinese province of Shaanxi, who fled from conflict and repression in the late 19th century. There are roughly 50,000 Kazakh citizens of Dungan ethnicity (as of 2010). Most Dungans are trilingual—a majority are Russian-speaking, and many also speak Dungan and/or one of the Central Asian languages. Dungans in Central Asia have been using their ability to act as intermediaries to initiate new forms of economic—as well as cultural—cooperation with China. This is not only in the sphere of bazaar trade and its associated service professions—it also involves initiatives such as the transfer of cutting-edge technologies and specialist training for workers.[61]

In the early years of the Central Asian states' independence, bazaar trade constituted a key site for people-to-people interactions with the Chinese. Its rapid growth and economic importance meant that cross-border trading relationships became an experience common to many Central Asians.

CONCLUSION

Relations between China and the Central Asian states strengthened rapidly following the latter countries' independence. Their cooperation on immediate issues such as border delimitation led to cooperation on the broader areas of investment and trade. China prioritized multilateral diplomacy in its relationships with the Central Asian states. The birth of the Shanghai Cooperation Organization (SCO) in 2001 marked an important step in this direction with the incorporation of regional bilateral relations into a multilateral negotiation framework. Diplomatically, the SCO set an important precedent for the BRI's approach to international relations, which likewise emphasizes multilateralism and high-level political dialogue.

China established a strong economic presence in Central Asian markets in sectors such as infrastructure, petroleum, mining and telecommunications. In many ways, China and the Central Asian states complement each other in terms of their economic needs. China's competitively priced products and services suit the economic position of Central Asian customers, whilst Central Asia provides international markets for Chinese goods and services. Chinese investment in infrastructure is also welcomed by the Central Asian states, since as small, low-income countries they struggle to provide the capital needed for major infrastructure projects. China began investing in infrastructure in Central Asia in the 1980s in order to facilitate cross-border trade, and it continued to invest throughout the 1990s and 2000s. China's participation in the infrastructure sector in the region, together with Chinese firms moving into other developing states, later inspired the massive investment in infrastructure backed by China's diplomatic and financial resources under the framework of the BRI.

As well as investment and cooperation at the state level, the BRI aims to strengthen social and cultural exchange. We have shown in this chapter that informal economic networks grew rapidly in the 1990s, leading to a thriving bazaar trade and numerous associated service professions that enabled goods to move across Eurasia. On both the state and interpersonal levels, then, the BRI represents the formalisation and scaling-up of a process that was already very much in motion.

NOTES

1. Qian Qichen zhidianxuanbu zhongguozhengfu chengren eluosil-ianbangzhengfu tongshi chengli wukelandeng shiyiguo duli [Qian Qichen dialled Russia Federation and other 11 post-USSR states and declared that the People's Republic of China government recognised their independence]. (1991, December 28). China Daily, p. 1.
2. Karrar, H. H. (2012). From Pastoral Nomadism to Shuttle Trading: A Long View of Commerce and Modernity Along the Sino-Central Asian Border. Material Culture, Language and Religion in Central and Inner Asia; Toronto Studies in Central and Inner Asia, No. 10, p. 207.
3. Mustafa, Z. (1969). The Sino-Soviet Border Problem. Pakistan Horizon, 22(4), 321–331. Retrieved from http://www.jstor.org/stable/41394679.
4. Laruelle, M., & Peyrouse, S. (2012). *The Chinese question in Central Asia: Domestic order, social change and the Chinese factor* (The comparative politics and international studies series). London: Hurst & Company, p. 15.
5. Laruelle & Peyrouse, p. 24.
6. Wu, H. (2005). Zhongya guojia he zhongguo de kuajing minzu rekou he fenbu[Central Asian countries and China's cross-border ethnicities]. World Ethno-National Studies, (5), 63–69. Retrieved from China National Knowledge Infrastructure: https://www.cnki.net/
7. Millward, J. A. (2007). *Eurasian crossroads: a history of Xinjiang.* *New York*: Columbia University Press.
8. Yuan, J. (2010). China's role in establishing and building the Shanghai Cooperation Organization (SCO). Journal of Contemporary China, 19(67), 855–869. doi: 10.1080/10670564.2010.508587
9. Cabestan, J. P. (2010). Central Asia-China relations and their relative weight in Chinese foreign policy. In Laruelle, M., Huchet, J.F., Peyrouse, S. & Balc, B. (Eds.). *China and India in Central Asia: A new great game*, New York: Palgrave Macmillan, pp. 25–40.
10. Millward, pp. 329–330.
11. Tumurkhuleg, T. (2012). Does the Shanghai Cooperation Organization represent an example of a military alliance? In Bedeski, R.E. and

Swantrom, N. (eds) *Eurasia Ascent in Energy and Geopolitics: Rivalry or Partnership for Russia, China and Central Asia?* Contemporary Asia Series. New York: Routledge, pp. 179–198.

12. Kalra, P., & Saxena, S. S. (2007). Shanghai Cooperation Organisation and Prospects of Development in Eurasia Region. Turkish Policy Quarterly, 6(2), 95–99.

13. Chung, C. P. (2006). China and the institutionalization of the Shanghai Cooperation Organization. Problems of Post-Communism, 53(5), 3–14.

14. Aris, S. (2011). Eurasian Regionalism: the Shanghai Cooperation Organization. London: Palgrave Macmillan, p. 22.

15. The Shanghai Cooperation Organisation, Declaration on the Establishment of the Shanghai Cooperation Organisation. Retrieved from the eng.sectsco.org.

16. Laruelle & Peyrouse, p. 28.

17. Laruelle & Peyrouse, p. 35.

18. Aris, S. (2011). *Eurasian Regionalism: the Shanghai Cooperation Organization.* London: Palgrave Macmillan, p. 30.

19. Brookes, P. (2006, June 12). Club For Dictators: An ugly agenda for Asia. The Heritage Foundation. Retrieved from https://www.heritage.org/defense/commentary/club-dictators-ugly-agenda-asia

20. J. Tkacik and A. Cohen. (2005). Sino-Russian military maneuvers: A threat to U.S. interests in Eurasia. Retrieved from https://www.heritage.org/europe/reportsino-russian-military-maneuvers-threat-us-interests-ineurasia.

21. Tumurkhuleg.

22. Song, W. (2014). Interests, power and China's difficult game in the Shanghai Cooperation Organization (SCO). Journal of Contemporary China, 23(85), 85–101. doi: 10.1080/10670564.2013.809981

23. Tolipov, F. (2004). On the role of the Central Asian Cooperation Organization within the SCO. Central Asia and the Caucasus, 27(3),146–154, retrieved from Cyberleninka https://cyberleninka.ru/

24. Fedholm, M. (2012). *The Shanghai Cooperation Organisation and Eurasian Geopolitics.* Copenhagen: NiAS Press, p. 250.

25. Karrar, H. (2013). Merchants, markets and the state: informality, *transnationality* and spatial imaginaries in the revival of Central Eurasian trade. *Critical Asian Studies, 45,* 459–80, p. 466.

26. National Bureau of Statistics of China.

27. Ibid.

28. Ibid.

29. Sadovskaya, Y. & Utyasheva, L. (2018). "Human Silk Road": The People-to-People Aspect of the Belt and Road Initiative. In Eds. Laruelle,

M. *China's Belt and Road Initiative and its impact in Central Asia*. Washington, D.C.: The George Washington University, Central Asia Program, 2018, p. 124.

30. Mogilevskii, R. (2019). Kyrgyzstan and the Belt and Road Initiative Kyrgyzstan and the Belt and Road Initiative (Working paper 50). Bishkek: Retrieved from https://www.ucentralasia.org/Content/downloads/UCA-IPPA-Wp50%20-%20ENG.pdf

31. Dreher, A., Fuchs, A., Parks, B.C., Strange, A. M., & Tierney, M. J. (2017). Aid, China, and Growth: Evidence from a New Global Development Finance Dataset (Aiddata working paper no.46). Williamsburg, VA:Aiddata.

32. Laruellle & Peyrouse, pp. 91–93.

33. Leung, G. C. (2010). China's oil use, 1990–2008. Energy policy, 38(2), 932-944. doi:10.1016/j.enpol.2009.10.045

34. Laruelle & Peyrouse, p. 72.

35. Movkebaeva, G. A. (2013). Energy cooperation among Kazakhstan, Russia, and China within the Shanghai cooperation organization. Russian Politics & Law, 51(1), 80–87. doi:10.2753/RUP1061-1940510105

36. Movkebaeva.

37. Kaminski, B., & Raballand, G. (2009). Entrepôt for Chinese Consumer Goods in Central Asia: The Puzzle of Re-exports through Kyrgyz Bazaars. *Eurasian Geography and Economics, 50*(5), 581–590.

38. Karrar, H. (2017). Kyrgyzstan's Dordoi and Kara-Suu Bazaars: Mobility, Globalization and Survival in Two Central Asian Markets. *Globalizations, 14*(4), 643–657, p. 653.

39. Gleason, G. (2003). *Market and politics in central Asia: Structural reform and political change*. London: Routledge, p. 65–6.

40. Cieślewska, A. (2014). From shuttle trader to businesswoman: the informal bazaar economy in Kyrgyzstan. In Morris, J. & Polese, A. *The informal post-socialist economy: Embedded practices and livelihoods*. London: Routledge, p. 121.

41. Ibid, p. 124.

42. Spector, R. (2017). *Order at the Bazaar: Power and Trade in Central Asia*. Ithaca, NY: Cornell University Press, p. 31.

43. Sadovskaya & Utyasheva, p. 115.

44. Spector, p. 25.

45. Alff, H. (2015). Profiteers or Moral Entrepreneurs?: Bazaars, Traders and Development Discourses in Almaty, Kazakhstan. *International Development Planning Review, 37*(3), 249–267, p. 258.

46. Spector, p. 27.

47. Karrar, p. 648.
48. Alff, H. (2016). Flowing goods, hardening borders? China's commercial expansion into Kyrgyzstan re-examined. *Eurasian Geography and Economics, 57*(3), 433–456, p. 441.
49. Sadovskaya and Utyasheva, p. 124.
50. Gleason, p. 63.
51. Ibid, p. 42.
52. Spector, p. 27.
53. Kaminski, B., & Raballand, G. (2009). Entrepôt for Chinese Consumer Goods in Central Asia: The Puzzle of Re-exports through Kyrgyz Bazaars. *Eurasian Geography and Economics, 50*(5), 581–590, p. 588.
54. Ibid.
55. Spector, p. 29.
56. Karrar, p. 644.
57. Spector, p. 28.
58. Laruelle, M., & Peyrouse, S. (2009). Cross-border Minorities as Cultural and Economic Mediators between China and Central Asia. *China & Eurasia Forum Quarterly, 7*(1).
59. Ibid.
60. Ibid, pp. 100–103.
61. Sadovskaya & Utyasheva, p. 117.

Chapter 4

THE BRI

Central Asian Case Studies

By the time that the BRI was announced in 2013, economic cooperation between Central Asia and China had been continually strengthening for over twenty years. This chapter asks how and to what extent the BRI has changed this relationship. It answers this question from two different perspectives. The first section gives a detailed discussion of the aims, mechanisms and institutions of the BRI, followed by case studies of specific projects which are underway in Central Asia. The second section looks at how the working lives of Central Asians in bazaar trade have been affected by increased economic cooperation with China. The focus on interaction at the interpersonal level adds an important dimension to the many commentaries on the BRI that centre around state-level cooperation. It also highlights how increased economic and social connectivity can create new forms of meaningful work.

THE BELT AND ROAD INITIATIVE: AIMS, MECHANISMS AND INSTITUTIONS

So far there is no official map of the BRI. The only Chinese government source that gives a sense of its proposed geographical coverage is the guideline document, "Vision and Actions on Jointly Building Silk Road Economic Belt and 21st Century Maritime Silk Road", which was published in March 2015. According to this document, the BRI consists of two megaprojects: the "Silk Road Economic Belt" (SREB), which links China with the Persian Gulf and the Mediterranean Sea through Central Asia and West Asia, and the "21st-Century Maritime Silk Road", for which one route is designed to go from China's coast to Europe through the South China Sea and the Indian Ocean, and the other through the South China Sea to the South Pacific.[1] According to this framework, the BRI spans 65 countries. The Chinese authorities have used the list of these 65 countries for BRI-related data collection. However, countries outside this list have also expressed their willingness to participate in the Initiative. As a result, from the end of 2015 onwards Chinese leaders have emphasised the openness of the BRI and have welcomed all countries to participate.[2]

China's proposal is to improve connectivity, and this includes cooperation in five areas: coordinating development policies; forging infrastructure and facilities networks; strengthening investment and trade relations; enhancing financial cooperation; and deepening social and cultural exchanges. The BRI prioritizes infrastructure development, looking to achieve the goal of connectivity through the construction of railways, ports, roads, power plants and transmission grids, and airports, as well as policy and financial support for those projects. However, the fact that the BRI is not clearly defined makes it difficult to identify what 'counts' as a BRI project. Most empirical studies tend to adopt a broad definition of BRI projects, whereby they include all Chinese investments in BRI countries after the proposal of the Initiative. Given this lack of clarity, estimates for the Belt and Road's size still vary dramatically after seven years since its proposal. One expert put its total cost at roughly $1tn;[3] whilst others are more sceptical and say that many of these commitments have not or will not be honoured, and that actual investments are closer to one third of that amount."[4]

China has created institutional structures under which the BRI projects can operate. It pledged $40bn to create its state-owned investment fund—the Silk Road Fund—in 2014 to support BRI projects. It has established a new multinational development bank, the Asian Infrastructure Investment Bank (AIIB), and has donated $2.98bn as capital to support infrastructure development in Asia. China's state banks and commercial banks are also providing loans for BRI projects and financial services for bilateral investment and trade between China and BRI states. The BRI financial institutions are seeking further cooperation with western partners as well as attracting capital flow from the private sector to spread the burden of funding those projects.[5] It is notable that although Chinese finance plays a leading role in funding the BRI projects, the institutional framework of BRI also includes other development banks and funds, such as the World Bank, the Asian Development Bank and the South-South Cooperation Assistance Fund.

Politically, the BRI represents China's bilateral and multilateral diplomacy across Eurasia and beyond. China has hosted the Belt and Road Forum for International Cooperation in 2017 and 2019, bringing dozens of government leaders from around the world to Beijing (29 and 37 state leaders attended in 2017 and 2019 respectively). A number of the bilateral and multilateral mechanisms already existing between China and the Eurasian states have also now been incorporated into the framework of the BRI. For instance, after the initiation of the BRI, the Shanghai Cooperation Organisation (SCO) meetings began to serve as a platform for the state leaders to discuss the possibility of connecting the agendas of the SCO and the BRI. As a result, in the Statement by the heads of government of the member states of the Shanghai Cooperation Organisation on Regional Cooperation, the heads of government officially confirmed for the first time their "support to the initiative of the People's Republic of China on the establishment of the Silk Road Economic Belt which shares the SCO development goals."[6]

China has worked to build a "synergy" between BRI projects, existing development initiatives and the agendas of countries in the region; for example, Kazakhstan's new economic policy, *Nurly Zhol* ("Bright Road"). Such synergy is based upon the overlap of the BRI's objectives with the national and regional initiatives of participant countries. The BRI also serves as a platform for other policy and financial cooperation projects which aim to improve connectivity in the region. For example, unimpeded trade and investment facilitation are core elements of the BRI and of the UN's 2030 Agenda for Sustainable Development, both of which emphasize the irreplaceable role of infrastructure in achieving sustainable development. The principle of inclusive and interconnected development forms the conceptual driving force for the synergy of the BRI with other cooperation initiatives.[7]

By August 2019, 136 countries and 30 international organizations had signed memorandum of cooperation or issued joint statements with China on building the Belt and Road together.[8] Although the cooperation documents take diverse forms, they all officially confirm the states' willingness to "jointly build the Belt and Road Initiative."

It is important to add here that China's domestic decision-making process plays an important role in how the BRI is implemented. This process, in terms of how projects are classified as 'BRI' and how budgets are allocated, is rarely discussed by commentators. The scholar Jie Yu asserts that China is not an authoritarian state where policies are dictated from the top—rather, policymaking is pluralistic.[9] Whilst the Standing Committee of the Chinese Communist Party and the State Council set long-term policy goals, specific policy measures are decided on and implemented by government ministries and state-owned enterprises. As a result, there are multiple political actors vying for influence. Although the workings of Chinese policy-making are not the focus of this book, it should be kept in mind that BRI projects are not the result of a monolithic state, but rather of competing interests within, as well as outside of, China.

CENTRAL ASIA IN THE BRI

Central Asia is of great significance in the Eurasian development program. The region lies at a central juncture within the Eurasian continent, which represents a strategic position given that the BRI seeks to link the European and Asian markets. In the era of the Ancient Silk Road, the region long served as the economic and trade hub for cross-regional business in the Eurasian continent. Two out of the six planned corridors of the land-based SREB go through Central Asia: China-Central Asia-Northern Europe (the New Eurasia Land Bridge) and China-Central Asia-West Asia. Central Asia also lies in between the China-Mongolia-Russia Economic Corridor and China-Pakistan Economic Corridor. If Central Asia were to be connected with Afghanistan and Pakistan through to the Arabian Sea, then the land 'belt' and the maritime 'road' would be joined up, bringing about integration of land and sea. Whilst, as discussed in the introduction, the notion of economic "corridors" does not accurately describe the reality of the BRI on the ground, the predominance of Central Asia within China's conceptualisation of the BRI nonetheless indicates that China considers it to be an important and strategic part of the Initiative.

As with several of the small, developing states along the SREB, the Central Asian states have suffered from their landlocked positions and are in need of transportation routes in order to connect with international markets. However, compared to some of the more turbulent BRI participants such as Pakistan and Afghanistan, Central Asian states possess a relatively stable political environment (though the recent disputed election and protests in Kyrgyzstan may have somewhat disrupted this stability). Furthermore, compared to some states in which China has invested little prior to the BRI, Chinese investment has entered the Central Asian markets since the 1990s and has encountered few problems. This has laid the ground for further Sino-Central Asian cooperation under the framework of BRI. In this sense, Central Asia could serve as the "demonstrative area" (*shi fan qu*) for the BRI, i.e. a region in which pioneering and successful projects are implemented, thus implying the feasibility of the Initiative.

As discussed in the introduction, Central Asia is also important for China's geopolitical interests. Roughly 3,300km of China's border is shared with Kazakhstan, Kyrgyzstan and Tajikistan, which accounts for over half the length of the international border of Xinjiang, China's largest administrative unit and frontier territory with a complex ethnic composition. The minorities in Xinjiang are also culturally and linguistically close with the people in Central Asian states. Islamist military groups from Central Asia have long supported the separatism of Xinjiang's Muslim Uyghurs. Therefore, the bilateral relationship with Central Asian states, as well as their development, is seen by China as important for the security and development of Xinjiang.

Central Asia's hydrocarbon resources are also of crucial importance to Beijing, regardless of the SREB's progress. China has built its first international oil pipeline which directly imports crude oil from Kazakhstan, where Chinese companies hold a significant stake in the oil sector. It has also built three lines of the Central Asia-China gas pipeline (CACGP) that runs from Turkmenistan via Uzbekistan and Kazakhstan to Khorgos in China's Xinjiang.[10] The construction of a fourth line is planned. According to the China National Petroleum Corporation, Chinese imports of Central Asian gas—mainly from Turkmenistan—account for over fifteen percent of total Chinese gas consumption, which ensures gas supply to about 300 million Chinese citizens.[11]

Some scholars also believe that Beijing is rebalancing its geopolitical strategy by strengthening its relations with its western neighbours in Central and South Asia. For example, Li Mingze, a Singaporean scholar, believes that the BRI constitutes a substantive move by China to "Act West."[12] The purpose of this is both to deal with disparate regional development and to avoid confrontation with the US following Washington's transfer of its focus in foreign policy from the Middle East to the Asia Pacific region.[13] This shift was brought in by the Obama administration and is known as

Washington's "Pivot to Asia." However, the Chinese government has adopted the term "Westward Development," thus emphasising development rather than geopolitical strategy.[14] Although scholars disagree on what China's exact geopolitical intention is, there is no doubt that China is strengthening its relations with its western neighbours on a large scale and that this at least has geopolitical implications. Central Asia is the starting point for such a move.

THE PRACTICE OF THE BRI IN CENTRAL ASIA

In some ways, the BRI marks a new stage of China-Central Asia relations, whilst in other ways it is a continuation. On the one hand, China has continued to develop a multinational institutional framework for the BRI, prioritising high-level diplomatic exchange and large-scale infrastructure investment. On the other hand, the scale of the cross-regional projects has been expanded under the BRI, and the projects have also been newly conceptualised as one element of China's larger international integration plan.

The BRI has become the most substantial content of China-Central Asia interaction, and it has begun to be clarified through consensus between the state leaders. Reaching such consensus happens via diverse bilateral and multilateral mechanisms, such as the Belt and Road Forum, the SCO's annual Council of Heads of State, and bilateral state visits. In 2013, Chinese President Xi paid visits to Uzbekistan, Kazakhstan, Turkmenistan and Kyrgyzstan. China established strategic partnerships with Kyrgyzstan and Turkmenistan during this visit, and has since established strategic partnerships with all five Central Asian nations. In 2017, presidents from Kazakhstan, Kyrgyzstan and Uzbekistan attended the first Belt and Road Forum in Beijing, and in 2019 the president of Tajikistan was also included in the attendance list.

The exchanges between state leaders have tended to result in vague but open statements that the two sides are willing to jointly build the Belt and Road Initiative. In 2018, the Kyrgyz president

Sooronbay Jeenbekov visited Beijing and the two sides agreed to establish a comprehensive strategic partnership. Jeenbekov stated that Kyrgyzstan was in support of the BRI, that he believed the initiative would "greatly promote common development in the region," and that Kyrgyzstan would "maintain the continuity of all cooperative agreements with China."[15] Similar statements have also been made by the presidents of Kazakhstan, Tajikistan and Uzbekistan.

In addition to their joint statement, China and Kazakhstan have also decided to establish connections between the BRI and Kazakhstan's domestic development program, as aforementioned. In 2014, Kazakhstan proposed its domestic economic stimulus program, *Nurly Zhol*, to improve its roads, railways and other infrastructure for sustainable and long-term growth. In 2015, Kazakhstan's President Nursultan Nazarbayev and President Xi released a Joint Declaration[16] stating their agreement that China's SREB and the economic policies proposed as part of Kazakhstan's Nurly Zhol complemented each other, and were conducive to deepening all-round cooperation between the two countries. Plans are also underway to link up the BRI and Tajikistan's domestic program, "National Planning and the 2030 Agenda for Sustainable Development in Tajikistan."

Apart from the common consensus reached between the state leaders, the head of the relevant ministry of both sides will reach a "Memorandum of Understanding" (MoU) to clarify the cooperation areas and principles. In cases of closer cooperation, working regimes are then established: these are multileveled, from the ministry level for setting cooperation agendas to civil society organisations— referred to in China as "social organisations"—as intermediate agencies between public and private sectors. Their activities also include the coordination of financial and policy support for the BRI projects. Notably, the government is seldom directly involved in the construction of the BRI projects. Instead, the intermediate social organizations are usually responsible for following up the projects with relevant firms and keeping the government updated.

The cooperation between Kazakhstan and China on industrial capacity is an example of this. The head of the National Development and Reform Commission of China (NDRC),[17] and the Ministry of Industry and Infrastructure Development of Kazakhstan (MIID) signed a bilateral framework agreement on strengthening cooperation on production capacity and investment. Based on this, the two sides then formed the China-Kazakhstan Coordination Cooperation Commission on Production Capacity and Investment, with the head of NDRC and MIID as Presidents of each side. Two secretariats as the permanent executive body of the Commission were established separately in the two administrative branches of the NDRC and MIID. The Chinese Overseas Development Association (CODA) and Kaznex-Invest were the social organizations registered and managed by the ministries. They served as the intermediate agencies between government and enterprises to coordinate their overseas investment activities. CODA and Kaznex-Invest worked together with enterprises to follow-up with the projects as well as formulating new projects. Financial services were also coordinated at this stage to support the relevant investment. In 2015, the two states announced the amalgamation of the two programs and Beijing pledged $2 billion to set up a capacity cooperation fund to support bilateral cooperation in industrial capacity, agricultural energy and regional connectivity projects. With the political and financial support mentioned above, specific projects are being created by firms on the market level. For example, China's state energy group, China National Petroleum Corporation (CNPC), and the Kazakh state oil and gas company KazMunaiGas jointly launched the renovation project of Shymkent Refinery, one of the three largest refineries in Kazakhstan.[18]

However, commentators have argued that on some matters, greater cooperation is required between China and the Central Asian countries. An example of this is the water supply issues arising from the fact that the two most important rivers for Kazakhstan's water supply are the Ili and Irtysh, both of whose sources lie in China. China's withdrawal of water from the rivers has resulted in water shortages in Kazakhstan, and the establishment of an industrial development zone in Xinjiang through which the river Ili passes has also led to its pollution by toxic substances. Negotiations between Kazakhstan and China on these issues have been ongoing for over a decade,[19] but with little progress, and critics have argued that these are complex issues that require greater compromise from both sides. The Irtysh basin is also shared by Russia: however, China is unwilling to engage multilaterally on this issue by including Russia in negotiations or by raising the issue at the SCO.[20] Whilst there are many positive examples of multilateral cooperation within the Eurasian space, there is certainly room for improvement, and China, as the most influential country within this region, is not always the perfect multilateral or bilateral negotiator.

THE IMPLEMENTATION OF BRI PROJECTS

The Chinese government does not report the BRI projects in a systematic way. Beyond headline investment numbers that have been announced by Chinese officials, and the occasional projection on intended country-level investment under the Initiative, BRI project information is not centrally reported.[21] Chinese policy banks and commercial banks sometimes make public announcements about project investment, and the media in China and the participant states also cover some BRI projects in their articles. Occasional presentations on some projects and government debt by government officials are also available in BRI states. As a result, for research purposes, researchers tend to identify specific BRI projects based on data drawn from official statistics, local and international media news, government press releases, interviews and reports.

The Central Asia Data-Gathering and Analysis Team (CADGAT) established by the Norwegian Institute of International Affairs (NUPI) and Bishkek's OSCE Academy identified 261 of China's BRI and bilateral projects in Central Asia. This list covers the projects launched after the first announcement of BRI in 2013 to January

2019. These projects are identified as BRI projects if they are publicly reported as BRI projects or if they are financed by the BRI-specific financial institutions: the Asian Infrastructure Investment Bank (AIIB), China's policy banks and the New Silk Road Fund. Otherwise, the project is simply identified as a normal bilateral project implemented in Central Asia.[22]

The infrastructure sector in Central Asia has been highly under-invested in due to the fact that infrastructure projects require long construction periods and are capital intensive. Cross-regional infrastructure such as railways and pipelines can connect the landlocked states to broader markets in Europe as well as East Asia. Central Asian states have been highly aware of their need and have been seeking investment from the international community. It seems possible that the BRI, with its massive investment in transport and energy infrastructure, will give the region an opportunity to revive something akin to its position on the ancient Silk Road, where Central Asia represented a focal point of trade within Eurasia and consisted of prosperous states and cities. However, some BRI projects have aroused local concerns on pollution, debt sustainability and insufficient knowledge transfer.

One significant example of a BRI project in Central Asia is the Sino-Kazakhstan International Logistics company at port Liangyungang on China's Eastern coast, which is a Kazakh-Chinese venture that became operational in 2015. Its neighbours are Japan and South Korea across the Pacific Ocean to the east, and westward it is connected to Kazakhstan via a railway running through China. The port is of significance for Kazakhstan and the other Central Asian states in enabling them for the first time to gain access to the Pacific Ocean. This was also facilitated by the opening in 2015 of the Khorgos Gateway, a dry port on the China-Kazakh border. The gateway is a key cargo hub along the Silk Road Economic Belt, and is used to transfer containers from Chinese trains to those on the Kazakh side (this is necessary because Chinese railways use a narrower gauge than the Kazakh railways, whose gauge is a legacy of

Sectors	Total number by sector	Kazakhstan	Kyrgyzstan	Tajikistan	Uzbekistan	Turkmenistan
Total by country	261	102	46	44	43	26
Trade and industrial development	131	61	17	17	24	12
Rail and road connectivity	51	14	11	16	5	5
Energy connectivity	48	20	5	7	12	4
People-to-people projects	31	7	13	4	2	5

Figure 4.1. Number of China's BRI projects and bilateral projects in Central Asia, by sector and country. Note that 'Trade and industrial development' covers projects in mineral and petroleum exploration, development and processing, industry, finance and IT, and agriculture and food. Source: Aminjonov, F., Abylkasymova, A., Aimée, A., Eshchanov, B., Moldokanov, D., Overland, I., & Valkulchuk, R. (2019). BRI in Central Asia: Overview of Chinese Projects. Central Asia Regional Data Review, 20, 1–5.

the Soviet period). The port has significantly increased the speed of goods transportation between China, Russia and Europe.[23]

New gas pipelines have also constituted major developments. In September 2014, construction work was begun on a new line of the pipeline running from Turkmenistan's giant gas fields all the way to the Chinese border through Uzbekistan, Tajikistan and Kyrgyzstan. Other infrastructure projects under construction and negotiation include the Western Europe-Western China highway (WEWC), the China-Kyrgyzstan-Uzbekistan railway, and the Trans-Asian Railway.

We now look in greater detail at two case studies of BRI projects in Central Asia: the Dushanbe-2 thermal power plant construction project in Tajikistan and the various BRI road projects in Kyrgyzstan.

Case Study I: Dushanbe-2 Thermal Power Plant Construction Project in Tajikistan

Tajikistan has long suffered from energy shortages. Hydropower plants generate ninety-five percent of all electricity in the country,[24] but these plants were built in Soviet times, and now, due to obsolete technology and lack of capital for rehabilitation, most of the power plants are facing a decrease in capacity. Acute electricity shortages often appear in winter, when water levels in rivers are low.[25] The

Tajik state-owned enterprise Barki Tojik, the owner of most of Tajikistan's power stations, launched a series of projects to address the issue.

One of these projects was to build a second thermal power plant—"Dushanbe-2"—in the capital, powered by coal and operating only in winter. Before the project started in 2012, Tajikistan had sought to secure funding from international concessional loan providers, but was frustrated. This was due to the fact that the plant only runs temporarily every year, and possibly also because it was not a renewable energy facility. Tajikistan was, however, subsequently able to secure funding from China. A memorandum of understanding to build the first phase of the project was reached between the Chinese electricity firm Tabian Apparatus StocCo (TBEA) and the Ministry of Energy and Industries of Tajikistan. The project consisted of two phases: phase 1 (constructed in 2012-2014) with installed capacity of 100MW and phase 2 (constructed in 2014-2016) with additional capacity of 300 MW. Phase 1 was financed by a $178 million loan from China's Eximbank. In return, the Tajik government granted the company access to gold deposits in Tajikistan in 2014. The contract to construct the second phase of the project was signed in 2014 at the SCO leader's summit in Dushanbe. The cost for the second phase was $349 million, of which $331 million was based on a highly concessional loan from Eximbank and $17.4 million from Barki Tojik. The construction of phase 2 started in 2015 and the leaders of Tajikistan and China attended the commencement ceremony.[26] Both of the phases have now been completed and Tajikistan is at the stage of paying back the loans. The plant is branded as "a model of the high-level cooperation between Tajikistan and China."

The plant is of great importance in solving the country's long-term problem of energy shortages in winter: it has enabled over 700,000 Dushanbe residents to regain central heating after 15 years of suspension.[27] However, there has been some opposition to the project. Complaints about the efficiency of the plant have been reported in the local media, as for most of the year, the power plant does not work at full capacity. The main concerns, though, relate to the environmental effects of the plant. It is located centrally within Dushanbe, and during the operation of the plant in 2014, local residents complained about soot deposited on their streets. According to TBEA, woven and electrical filtration systems were installed at the plant in order to ensure low combustion emissions into the atmosphere,[28] but several other sources claimed that these quality filters had not actually been installed. Local environmental groups have maintained concerns over the environmental impacts of using coal, and several official agencies in Tajikistan were against the project from the outset, such as the Environmental Protection Agency and three of the government ministries.[29]

This case study demonstrates the complexity of BRI projects on the ground. This perspective contrasts with the mainstream literature on the BRI, which focuses on China's geo-economic interests in the participant states of BRI. The Dushanbe-2 project is of particular interest as the agreement to go ahead with it was reached under the SCO framework, but it was branded as a BRI project after the proposal of the BRI. This implies that the BRI represents the evolution of Chinese overseas investment and diplomacy, instead of an alarming brand-new strategy. Tajikistan has long been aware of its needs for infrastructure development. Compared to the help from international development institutions, loans from Chinese development banks are sometimes not only highly concessional but also impose lower requirements for the project. As mentioned in the case above, Tajikistan found it nearly impossible to secure funds from international institutions. This meant that the Chinese loan was Tajikistan's best, or even sole, option. Funds from China therefore offer much-needed alternatives to the current international development finance that is available for infrastructure development in states like Tajikistan. At the same time, however, the fact that the Chinese loan for this project was not conditional on environmental standards is troubling, and clearly caused significant local and national resistance to the project.

Case Study II: BRI in Kyrgyzstan: Road to Debt or Glorious Future?

China became the largest source of foreign direct investment (FDI) into Kyrgyzstan from 2012. According to Professor Roman Mogilevsky of the University of Central Asia in Bishkek, the inward Chinese FDI to Kyrgyz Republic from 2006–2017 was equal to $2.3 billion, equivalent to between twenty-five and fifty percent of total FDI to the state.[30] In his report *Kyrgyzstan and the Belt and Road Initiative,* Mogilevsky identified 12 major infrastructure projects financed by China and implemented by Chinese contractors in Kyrgyzstan. He found that for 2011-2017—the period in which China-financed infrastructure was most actively implemented—$2.2 billion was spent on infrastructure projects and $1.9 billion on FDI projects.[31]

The above investment is equivalent to some seven to eight percent of GDP per annum—a substantial portion of the Kyrgyz economy. However, Mogilevsky observes that since many of these resources were spent on the importation of goods and services from China, the main impact on Kyrgyz GDP is likely to be through the accumulation of physical capital such as improved roads and electricity transmission lines. There are also tax contributions, of course: in 2017, enterprises connected to China paid around $53.2 million to the government of Kyrgyzstan in taxes.[32] It is a prevalent assumption amongst media and other commentators that these projects contribute little to local employment as they are implemented by Chinese companies hiring mostly Chinese nationals and a very limited number of local workers.[33] However, Dirk van der Kley has presented evidence that somewhat challenges this assumption. Based on a range of information sources such as interviews with workers, site observations and company shareholder minutes, van der Kley argues that for major projects in Kyrgyzstan and Tajikistan, Chinese investors and contractors are actively trying to localise their workforce, and in many cases Chinese companies are employing a majority of local workers.[34] In any case, improved infrastructure also benefits other workers in a wide range of occupations, such as those in trade. The massive investment in infrastructure projects has also aroused concern around Kyrgyzstan's external debts. China's policy bank, the Export-Import (Exim) Bank of China, is the Kyrgyz government's largest creditor. The government's debts owed to the bank have risen from $9 million in 2008 to $1.7 billion in 2017, consisting of forty-two percent of total external debt or twenty-four percent of Kyrgyzstan's GDP. The question of how to repay this debt could become a pressing one: Mogilevsky suggests that "the debt service burden may start to be felt after the expiration of the grace period for most loans (in the 2020s)."[35] Mogilevsky also points out, however, that the Exim Bank's interest rates of 1.86%–2.5% make it far cheaper to borrow from China than from local banks, where interest is about five times higher.[36] It is also worth noting that not all of the projects are financed by loans. In the early stages of the rehabilitation of the Osh-Sarytash-Irkeshtam road, part of this project was financed through a "resources in exchange for investments" scheme, whereby Kyrgyzstan allowed a Chinese mining company to develop a Kyrgyz gold deposit (discussed in chapter 3).[37] The most recent project funded by the Exim Bank was the rehabilitation of the street network in Bishkek, enabled by two grants totalling $121 million: by asking for grants instead of loans, the Kyrgyz government signalled its effort to ease public concern over debt pressure from China.[38]

Mogilevsky lists five road construction and rehabilitation projects funded up Chinese loans: the Bishkek-Naryn-Torugart road rehabilitation project, the alternative North-South road project (connecting the capital Bishkek with Kyrgyzstan's biggest southern city, Osh), the rehabilitation of the Osh-Sarytash-Irkeshtam road, the Osh-Batken-Isfana road, and the rehabilitation of street networks in Bishkek.[39] These projects have been simultaneously understood as constituting "corridors" with a programme called Central Asia Regional Economic Cooperation (CAREC). CAREC was established by the Asian Development Bank (ADB), a US-Japan backed regional development bank, to encourage economic cooperation among countries in the

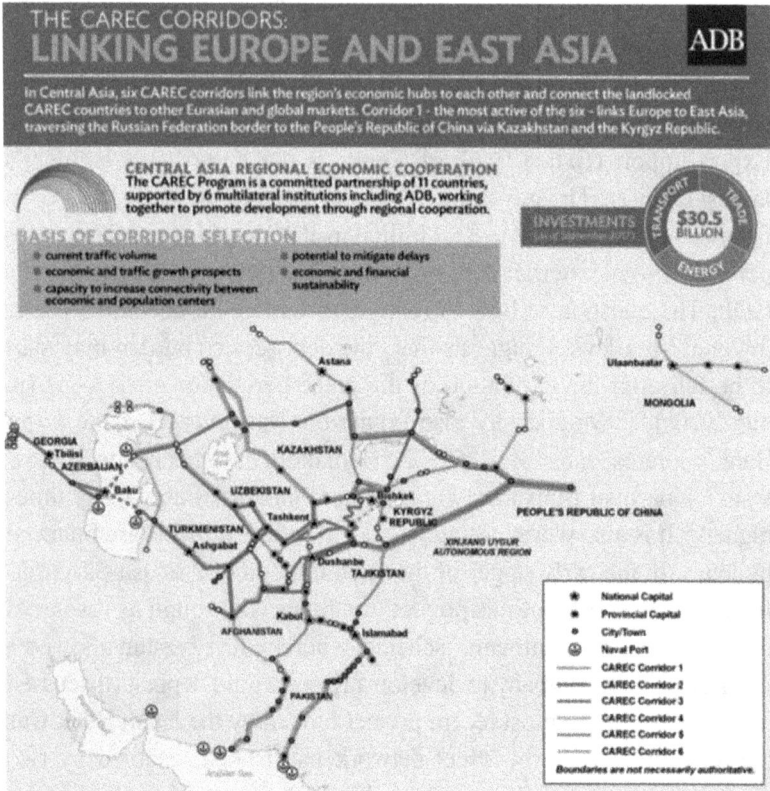

Figure 4.2.   **CAREC corridors.** Source: Aminjonov, F., Abylkasymova, A., Aimée, A., Eshchanov, B., Moldokanov, D., Overland, I., & Valkulchuk, R. (2019). BRI in Central Asia: Overview of Chinese Projects. Central Asia Regional Data Review, 20, 1–5.

Central Asian region. Six CAREC corridors in the program have been planned in order to improve the transportation links in Central Asia and connect the region with its neighbours (Fig. 4.2).

With the exception of the China-aided road project to develop the street network in Bishkek, China is not the only creditor for any of these projects. Instead, China's development banks sponsor sections of the road, whilst other international development institutions, such as the World Bank or the Asian Development Bank, cover the remaining cost. For example, the Kyrgyz government

Table 4.1. Financing the Osh-Batken-Isfana Road. Mogilevsky, R. (2019). Kyrgyzstan and the Belt and Road Initiative.

Section of road	Donor	Financing	Payback period	Grace Period	Rate of interest (Grace Period)	Rate of interest	Contractor
10–28km	WB	$16m, comprised of $8.8m loan and $7.2m grant	40 years	10 years			Xinjiang-Bei xin
28–75km	JICA	$75m	40 years	10 years	0.1%		Japan-tied procurement
75–108km	IsDB	$21.32m					CRBC
108–123 km.	EU	€14.9m grant					CRBC
248–271 km, binder course. Completed							
123–155 km. Completed	WB	$25m	40 years	10 years	0,5% - 0,75% -		Xinjiang-Bei xin
155–220 km. Completed	EBRD	$35m	20 years	5 years	1% (variable)		Xinjiang-Bei xin
220–232 km, 271–360 km, 248–271 km, wearing course. Completed.	Exim Bank	$91.46m	20 years	9 years		2%	CRBC

has sought funding for the Osh-Batken-Isfana road construction project from multiple development institutions. They have gained two grants totalling €14.9 million from the European Union, and several other development institutions also pledged concessional loans to finance the project. Japan's governmental development assistance body—the Japan International Cooperation Agency—signed a loan agreement with the Government of the Kyrgyz Republic to provide a Japanese Official Development Assistance (ODA) loan of up to 11.915 billion yen for the 28-75 km stretch of the road with Japanese procurement. China's Exim Bank provided in total $91.46 million to finance three sections of the road. Except for a minor part of the project where contracting information is not available, nearly all of the Exim-financed road was constructed by two Chinese transport engineering firms, the China Road and Bridge Corporation and the Xinjiang Beixin Road & Bridge group. Most of the construction work was finished between 2016 and 2018.[40] Table 4.1 is taken from Kyrgyz government records, and shows how the Osh-Batken-Isfana road was financed by a range of institutions.

The Osh-Batken-Isfana road project is fulfilling a pre-existing Kyrgyz development aim to build a reliable road from Osh to its border with Tajikistan and Uzbekistan in Fergana Valley. The 360km-long road includes both new construction and rehabilitation, such as repairs to rural roads in the Batken region. It winds its way through the Ferghana Valley, linking the remote but fertile areas in southwest Kyrgyzstan with Osh, the southern capital and the second largest city in the country. The road connects up eighteen percent of the Kyrgyz population.[41] Before the rehabilitation, the road was in poor condition: it sent clouds of harmful dust over nearby areas in the summer, and during the winter months cars would get stuck in mud. Routes previously had to pass through Uzbek and Tajik territory, which necessitated the time-consuming process of crossing borders. As the new road has started to take shape, travel times have been significantly reduced, and the increased traffic has encouraged local businesses such as coffee shops and small markets to establish themselves along the road.[42] The road provides potential transit traffic to and from Tajikistan, and connects Kyrgyzstan with international transport corridors to Kazakhstan and Russian. As with the Dushanbe-2 project in Tajikistan, the road projects in the Kyrgyz Republic were proposed in its national program. Along with the multiple international development banks, China is one of several creditors for the project. Given this, it is misleading to brand all BRI road projects as "Chinese" roads, implying that China is the only actor enabling these projects to happen. However, China's funding does stand out compared to loans from the World Bank or Asian Development Bank. The primary reason lies in the fact that the institutional framework used by Chinese institutions to implement these infrastructure projects is highly dependent upon negotiation with the other participants involved in the project. This flexibility means that projects are more likely to come to fruition than if strict regulations had been applied, since the partners can take creative approaches to solve problems. An example of this is the investment in exchange for resources in phase 1 of the Dushanbe-2 thermal power plant construction project.

However, there is a concerning lack of transparency regarding the details of these agreements, largely due to China being slow to publish information about Chinese oversea lending, especially information in English. This approach arouses suspicions about the possibility of unknown deals being involved in the projects. China-financed projects are sometimes criticised for giving priority to Chinese contractors, which often limits the involvement of international competitors. This kind of tied procurement was also an issue in the case of the Japanese financing for the Osh-Batken-Isfana road in Kyrgyzstan.

Of course, it may be premature to clearly define the characteristics of China's institutional approach to financing BRI projects based only on these two cases from Tajikistan and the Kyrgyz Republic. Nonetheless, for the research purposes of this book, these cases are enough to show the complex nature of the BRI projects, and to show that these projects are already listed on the participant states' own development agenda, rather than being a Chinese conception. Sometimes the projects are sponsored by Chinese credit only, but very often the projects are financed by China along with international development banks, meaning that China's role in these projects should not be exaggerated. We would therefore warn against taking an overly China-centric approach when constructing narratives about the BRI. These case studies suggest to researchers and commentators the importance of incorporating the development agendas of BRI states, as well as their interaction with international development institutions, into the overall picture about how the BRI functions in practice.

LOCAL ATTITUDES TOWARDS CHINESE PRESENCE IN CENTRAL ASIA

As well as looking at the operation of BRI projects on the ground, it is important to consider how Central Asians view the increasing importance of China in Central Asia. Whilst Central Asian leaders and elites tend to view increased cooperation with China as overall a positive development, this does not always correspond with the views of ordinary citizens in the region. Fears of China mainly centre around increased Chinese migration, rather than Chinese investment per se. This is partly due to existing problems such as local manufacturers struggling to compete with the influx of cheap Chinese goods.[43] However, the media and some political actors also exacerbate this fear, often emphasising the huge imbalance in population size between the two regions: one local newspaper wrote that "the enormous difference in the size of the two countries and peoples would mean that the Kyrgyz would soon drown in a Chinese sea."[44]

The local reaction to Chinese presence is shaped by a number of factors. For those who have had little interaction with the Chinese, attitudes remain heavily influenced by the historical legacy of Sino-Soviet relations, with old clichés of Soviet propaganda casting China as the enemy. Discourses on "Chinese expansion" into Central Asia are common in Kazakh, Kyrgyz and Tajik newspapers. There are two very widespread preconceptions about China: firstly, that China does not change over time and pursues objectives which stretch across several centuries or even millennia, and secondly, that the Chinese authorities harbour concealed imperialist intentions.[45] Alarmist views are heightened by the lack of both popular and academic knowledge of China in the region.

Views may also be shaped by global concerns about the BRI. As we mentioned in the introduction, there is internationally widespread concern about the accumulation of debt by those states in which BRI projects are carried out. The notion of the "debt-trap" was for the most part introduced by South Asian writers referring to Sri Lanka's Hambantota port, where Sri Lanka handed the control of the port to a Chinese state-owned enterprise on a ninety-nine-year lease. The debt-trap theory was later adopted by some U.S. think tanks, popularized by mainstream media, and echoed by politicians across the world.[46] However, Deborah Brautigam of Johns Hopkins University argues that of more than 3,000 China-financed projects that she and others have tracked, Hambantota is the only one that is used by critics to evidence the debt-trap theory. It is the exception, not the rule.[47]

In Kyrgyzstan, Kazakhstan, and to a lesser extent Tajikistan, anti-Chinese sentiment has led to protests. From December 2018 to January 2019, three rallies took place in the centre of Bishkek. Activists gathered to protest against the increasing number of Chinese labour migrants in Kyrgyzstan. They demanded that "illegal" migrants be deported, and also that the Kyrgyz government would cancel its debt to China. The protests were initiated by a nationalist group called Kyrk Choro (Forty Knights), an initiative which aims to "raise the young generation as patriots, to protect Kyrgyz values, our culture and language." One of the organisers of the rally stated that "people are angry that we mostly use Chinese labour, and there are very few Kyrgyz workers building our roads."[48] It is difficult to discern how much appeal these values have among the broader population.[49] In Kazakhstan, the possibility that the Kazakh government might rent the country's farmland to China has also given rise to major protests. In an attempt to prevent similar incidents in their own countries, Uzbekistan and Turkmenistan have introduced strict limits on the number of Chinese migrants that can be employed locally.[50]

Attitudes towards China in Central Asia are, however, highly varied, and several surveys have cast light on this. A representative sociological study carried out in Kazakhstan in 2007 and 2012 found that attitudes towards Chinese presence varied by region.[51] Two regions—eastern and central Kazakhstan—saw a significant increase from 2007 to 2012 in positive attitudes towards Chinese presence.[52] In eastern Kazakhstan, 93% of respondents had a neutral or positive attitude towards the Chinese in 2012. The scholars Yelena Sadovskaya and Leah Utyasheva suggest that in the eastern region this is probably due to increased economic ties with Xinjiang.[53]

As Sadovskaya and Utyasheva point out, negative attitudes towards the 'other' are likely to change for those Central Asians who have begun to collaborate more frequently with the Chinese.[54] The question of how Central Asians are experiencing the increased Chinese presence requires an on-the-ground perspective. In the next section, we take this perspective by drawing upon ethnographic studies of bazaar traders in Kyrgyzstan and Kazakhstan in order to explore China-Central Asia relations on an interpersonal level. Of course, perceptions of China are various, complicated and difficult to measure: these case studies do not by any means provide a comprehensive summary of attitudes. Rather, by examining the specific case of bazaar trade, they add richness and context to our preceding discussion of relations between China and Central Asia at the state and institutional level. Importantly, they show how state-level policies on international cooperation can affect individuals and their working lives.

THE BRI AND WORKING LIVES: BAZAAR TRADE IN KYRGYZSTAN AND KAZAKHSTAN

As discussed, China's aim to improve overall connectivity includes cooperation in five areas, the fifth of which is the deepening of social and cultural exchanges. In the following section we focus upon this area, which has received the least attention from commentators of the five. Attention is merited, however, since increasing interpersonal connections will facilitate greater cooperation in the other four areas too. Enhancing people-to-people bonds is central to the Chinese vision of the "New Silk Roads" and of a world order which prioritises mutual understanding, connectivity and peaceful coexistence.

This section draws on case study evidence to show the importance of people-to-people connections to the present-day relationship between China and Central Asia. It was primarily cross-border traders from the 1980s onwards who were responsible for reinitiating regular people-to-people interactions between China and Central Asia.[55] For this reason, this book uses bazaar trade as a case study, as it has been the predominant sphere of interpersonal economic interaction between the two regions. The case studies used here look at the relationships formed by bazaar traders in Kyrgyzstan and Kazakhstan with Chinese business partners. Kyrgyzstan and Kazakhstan have been chosen as case studies within the Central Asian region because there is a larger body of literature on bazaar trade in these countries relative to the other Central Asian countries. As discussed in chapter 3, this is due to Kyrgyzstan and Kazakhstan having pursued the most open trade policies of these countries since independence and therefore being subject to the greatest quantities of transnational bazaar trade.[56]

The case study evidence also demonstrates how cross-border trade policies affect traders' experience of work. Asking how, or whether, people value their work is a question of central importance in gaining insight into their daily lives. In evaluating people's experience of work, we should not only consider material rewards but also whether that work is a source of self-respect and pride.[57]

One of Central Asia's biggest bazaars is Dordoi, a covered market on the outskirts of Bishkek which provides employment to over 40,000 people. One of the authors made a brief visit to Dordoi bazaar in 2018, so we will begin with a few observations of the Dordoi bazaar in order to give a sense of the setting. It should be kept in mind, however, that bazaars are very much *not* static institutions: their embeddedness in global networks of commerce means that they are constantly changing. This description is from a particular point in time, and things will have changed since that point, and likewise since the time periods in which the case studies were carried out.

At the time of the author's visit, there were a roughly even mix of men and women trading in the bazaar: women were mainly at the stalls selling food, shoes, and women's clothing, whilst appliances, electronics, mechanical goods and men's clothing tend to be sold by men. The infrastructure of the bazaar consisted predominantly of rows of blue shipping containers, double-stacked, with the bottom container used for displaying goods and the top for storage. Advertisements, in a mixture of Cyrillic and Latin script, hung on banners from the ceiling. The largest sections of the bazaar were dedicated to shoes and clothing, but there was a huge array of different consumer goods on offer; everything from garden tools to foodstuffs to lighting. According to a Kyrgyz friend, goods from different countries were sold in different parts of the bazaar, and Chinese goods were cheaper and poorer quality than goods from Turkey or locations in Europe. It seemed that there was a widely-perceived hierarchy of goods according to their geographical origin.

Many of the traders in Kazakh and Kyrgyz bazaars were migrants, including Tajiks, Uyghurs, Russians and Han-Chinese. The range of ethnicities present at the bazaar was evident from the different cuisines available, although as in most restaurants in Kyrgyzstan, Kyrgyz, Uzbek and Uyghur cuisines were offered together and presented as "the national dishes." There was also a pop-up stall where visitors could buy a cappuccino: this, according to a friend who had lived in Bishkek, was a new addition at the time of the visit. There were several stalls selling Kyrgyz textiles: these were common in Dordoi as the textiles industry had recently been growing in Bishkek. Most often, fabrics are imported from China and used for apparel production in small-to-medium-sized factories in the Kyrgyz capital.[58]

As discussed in chapter 3, many of the goods sold at Dordoi bazaar are Chinese. The question of how bazaar traders experience their interactions with Chinese business-people is addressed by anthropologists Henryk Alff and Magnus Marsden. Two of Alff's case studies draw upon ethnographic research carried out in bazaars and based on interviews with traders. The first deals with wholesale traders at the Bolashak bazaar in the city of Almaty, Kazakhstan.[59] The Bolashak bazaar is part of the larger Barakholka bazaar agglomeration. The case study focuses particularly upon a couple, Alina and Farhad, who worked as traders from the time of the bazaar's establishment in the early 1990s. Alina started off by purchasing Chinese-made consumer goods from a Han-Chinese wholesaler at the Bolashak bazaar and reselling them at a higher price. She and Farhad now have a wholesale fashion business: they design clothing with their Chinese partners, who manufacture it in Beijing. The couple then import this clothing in bulk and redistribute it to retailers in other parts of Kazakhstan and Western Siberia.[60]

The second case study uses Alff's interviews with a range of traders at the Dordoi bazaar, all of whom are involved in some way in trade relations with China.[61] Alff examines how traders view their exchange activities with China in the run-up to Kyrgyzstan's potential accession to the Eurasian Economic Union (EAEU) (which occurred in 2015).

In both case studies, Alff observes that traders attribute value to their long-term relationships with Chinese business partners. For many wholesale traders in Dordoi, successful trade is "about actively building and maintaining trustworthy connections" with these partners.[62] From Alff's evidence it can be observed that in Dordoi and Bolashak these relationships have three dimensions to them which are of value to traders.

The first is learning to communicate effectively with the Chinese. Over the years that Alina and Farhad have been trading with Chinese business-people, they have developed a basic proficiency in the Chinese language as well as intercultural communication skills and experience in negotiation. They see these skills as enabling them to build relationships of "mutual reliability . . . across social, ethnic and spatial boundaries."[63] It is clear that they value personal communication, since Alina travels to Beijing several times a year to meet and liaise with the manufacturers there from whom she imports clothing. For the couple, the capacity to build reliable relationships across borders constitutes sophisticated entrepreneurship. Likewise, in Dordoi, some of the more experienced traders refer to knowledge of the Chinese language and intercultural understanding as a way of "staying competitive."[64]

The second dimension stems from a widespread admiration of the Chinese business etiquette. Traders perceive that useful business skills can be learnt from cooperation with the Chinese. One Russian trader at Dordoi said that she had learnt how to adapt production to demand through working with Chinese partners. Another Dordoi trader perceived that successful entrepreneurship was about adopting Chinese approaches to trade, such as flexibility and innovativeness.[65] Alff suggests that this appreciation of Chinese business practices is connected to a respect for "Chinese modernity": traders emphasise China's "rapid infrastructural transformation" and the pragmatism exhibited by the Chinese in doing business.[66]

Finally, traders value these reliable, long-term relationships because they enable them to cope with the uncertain conditions of everyday business activities. Since written contracts seldom feature in determining rules for business conduct in bazaar trade, trust is essential for establishing predictability. One pertinent example of this is Kyrgyzstan's 2015 accession to the EAEU. In the run-up to this development, traders knew that Kyrgyzstan's incorporation would mean the removal of its trade barriers with Kazakhstan, but more expensive imports from China.[67] This was a cause for considerable anxiety amongst many Dordoi traders. However, some traders were more optimistic, hoping that due to their long-standing relationships with Chinese business partners, the latter would lower the prices of their goods so that they could continue working with traders in Kyrgyzstan. In this regard, one Russian garment wholesaler observed: "'I have been working with Chinese partners for five years . . . We have gotten a sense of how to cooperate with them, and we know that they are eager to stay in business relations with us'."[68]

Relevant to the study of these transnational relationships is the work of the anthropologist Magnus Marsden, who has carried out ethnographic research into traders of Afghan background who operate in China, Central Asia, Russia and the Ukraine. Though Afghans come from a country context that differs from Kyrgyzstan and Kazakhstan in important ways—notably, being war-torn and having been occupied by Soviet forces rather than part of the Soviet Union—they inhabit many of the same trading networks as traders in these countries. Marsden's work on how Afghan traders speak about their livelihoods serves as a comparison to demonstrate how the values held by traders in Dordoi and Bolashak are likely to have wider relevance across the region. Like the traders in Dordoi and Bolashak, Afghan traders belong to far-reaching transnational networks involving the transport and sale of consumer goods. They therefore have to interact with people from a range of nationalities and ethnicities. Marsden observes that Afghan traders refer to themselves as "diplomats" in terms of the skills they require to trade successfully. They "take pride" in presenting themselves as having the right knowledge and skills to "navigate myriad and complex forms of international relations, boundaries and divisions."[69] They particularly emphasise their ability to be flexible in the sense of speaking multiple languages and adapting to diverse cultural settings. The similarities with Alff's observations in Dordoi and Bolashak are striking: this suggests the possibility that these are commonly shared values amongst transnational traders in the Eurasian region.

Not only do traders value these dependencies, but they also frequently emphasise that transnational relationships and trust are what *enables* trade to happen. For Alina and Farhad, the trust generated through everyday maintenance of relationships is "the driving force making trans-continental trade and transport actually work."[70] The personalisation of trade relations has often been associated with the informal economy and seen as an inhibitor to the efficient functioning of the market. However, this viewpoint is countered by the traders' observations that the flow of goods simply would not happen without interpersonal relations. This has broader implications for our understanding of how cross-border trade works.

From looking at formal trade statistics, Kyrgyzstan appears to occupy a liminal position with respect to global capitalism. However, this is due to the fact that most of its imports and exports go through non-standard channels and therefore do not show up in these statistics. The scholar Hasan Karrar makes the argument that, in fact, Kyrgyzstan plays an essential role in global capitalism since it allows goods to be re-exported from China to other Eurasian destinations: he points out that "if shoes manufactured in Guangzhou end up in a wholesale market in Moscow via Dordoi, then Kyrgyzstan is not as peripheral as it may appear."[71]

We might therefore see bazaar trade as central to Eurasian transnational trade and therefore to the BRI, rather than as an exception to "formal" trade practices. Too often, accounts of the BRI only examine bilateral trade deals between China and its neighbours at the state level without looking at the movement of goods through bazaars. A more complete picture of trade in Eurasia is attained through a consideration of bazaar trade, providing a greater understanding of the context within which BRI came about and is being enacted.

This section has shown that transnational relationships with Chinese traders have become a source of value for workers in Central Asian bazaars. Our focus on a relatively small number of bazaar traders does, of course, limit the scope of our insights. It should also be noted that increased Chinese presence has had detrimental effects on other types of work in Central Asia. For example, major Chinese companies such as the CNPC bring their equipment from China, meaning that local entrepreneurs are unable to sell to them. Chinese companies have also built up a reputation in Kyrgyzstan and Kazakhstan for neglecting workers' rights.[72] And as discussed previously, distrust also exists in many cases between Chinese and Central Asians.

However, we do not aim to draw conclusions about the effect of the BRI on the livelihoods of all Central Asians. Rather, the perspective we have adopted brings us to a different way of thinking about multilateral trade cooperation by considering the value that it can bring to workers. The value of this cooperation is not only in security and economic prosperity: there is also social value in building cross-border relationships. China has recognised the importance of this through its inclusion of social and cultural exchange in its five areas of cooperation. The increased economic connectivity under the BRI can therefore be understood as contributing to the creation of particular forms of work based around transnational relationships. These have long been in existence, but have seen marked growth since the 1990s. Whilst, as discussed in chapter 3, bazaar trading was initially a widespread survival strategy, for many traders it has come over time to acquire meanings that go beyond this. The continued expansion of infrastructure and trade connections between China and Central Asia under the BRI is likely to create more opportunities for meaningful work and cross-border relationships. For much of Central Asia's history, mobility has been a central element of livelihoods. It is once again becoming an important part of the social fabric of the region.

CONCLUSION

This chapter has shown that cooperation is a defining feature of the BRI, at both the state and the interpersonal level. The BRI's implementation in Central Asia does not constitute an entirely top-down intervention by the Chinese. On the state level, the agendas of existing multilateral institutions, such as the SCO and the EAEU, have become incorporated into the BRI. Of course, China is clearly the more powerful actor in its relationships with Central Asia. Nonetheless, the BRI projects are by their nature collaborative, since they form part of the development paradigm of the BRI states and are aligned with the existing policy aims of these countries.

As shown by the case study of the Tajik power plant project and the Kyrgyz road project, China also plays an important role in complementing international institutions to finance BRI projects. The creativity of Chinese financing arrangements is attractive to Central Asian countries who may struggle to secure funds from elsewhere, though the lack of environmental conditions attached to these loans is a cause for concern.

This chapter goes some way towards answering the question posed at the beginning of the chapter: how is the BRI changing the nature of the Sino-Central Asian relationship? As shown in chapter 3, China's investment in infrastructure and hydrocarbon projects, and its desire to facilitate trade, have been present in Central Asia long before the BRI. On the other hand, though, the BRI has been accompanied by a ramping up of China's diplomatic and economic activities in the region. With the proposal of the Initiative, a clearer financial and institutional framework was developed for projects, including for example the birth of AIIB and the Belt and Road Forum.

This chapter provides readers with a new perspective on the BRI by looking at the facts of BRI projects on the ground. Against the current narrative of the BRI as China's grand strategy, we propose here that commentary about the BRI should recognise that states participating in the BRI are implementing projects according to their own development agendas, and that as a result they have more agency and choice than is often acknowledged. We also emphasise that BRI projects are enabled by multiple international development institutions and not only by Chinese ones. This approach is emblematic of the idea of the "Open Left," discussed in our introduction: it consists of a multilateralism which involves non-western actors and which is based upon engagement with policy ideas from a wide variety of countries.

Finally, we have observed that cooperation between Central Asia and China is also happening at the interpersonal level, which forms an important and often neglected element of the BRI. Relationships of trust between Central Asian and Chinese traders have underpinned the ongoing movement of bazaar-traded goods across Eurasia. As Beijing has understood since the 1980s, cross-border trade cooperation between China and Central Asia is important in helping to bring peace and prosperity to Central Asia and to the Western regions of China. However, our case studies suggest that there is social value in trade cooperation too: for those who work in bazaar trade, building strong trading relationships across borders is a source of pride and meaning. The facilitation of cross-border trade and multilateral trade agreements under the BRI is likely to bring benefits beyond economic gains.

NOTES

1. National Development and Reform Commission (NDRC), & Foreign Ministry and Ministry of Commerce (with approval by the State Council) (2015n). Vision and action for jointly building the silk road Economic Belt and the 21st century maritime silk road. Bo'ao forum, March 2015, Hainan.
2. The Belt and Road Portal. (2019, April 25). Yidai yilu zhongde dai-helu zaina [Where is the "Belt" and "Road" in the Belt and Road Initiative]. Retrieved from https://ishare.ifeng.com/c/s/7mA5UOHZjG5
3. Perlez, J., & Huang, Y. (2017). Behind China's $1 trillion plan to shake up the economic order. New York Times. Retrieved from https://www.nytimes.com/2017/05/13/business/china-railway-one-belt-one-road-1-trillion-plan.html
4. Joy-Pérez, C., & Scissors, D. (2018). Be Wary of Spending on the Belt and Road. Washington D.C.: American Enterprise Institute. Retrieved from http://www.aei.org/publication/be-wary-of-spending-on-the-belt-and-road/
5. Kynge, J., Hornby, L., & Weinland, D. (2018, July 16). China development banks expand links with foreign lenders. Financial Times. Retrieved from https://www.ft.com/content/e0a2dd52-85b4-11e8-a29d-73e3d454535d
6. The Shanghai Cooperation Organisation (2014). Statement by the heads of government (prime ministers) of the member states of the Shanghai Cooperation Organization on regional economic cooperation. Zhengzhou: China. Retrieved from the Shanghai Cooperation Organisation. http://eng.sectsco.org/
7. Cai, F., & Nolan, P. (Eds). (2019). *Routledge Handbook of the Belt and Road*. London: Routledge, p. 189.
8. Liu, W., Zhang, Y., & Xiong, W. (2020). Financing the Belt and Road Initiative. Eurasian Geography and Economics, 61(2), 137–145. https://doi.org/10.1080/15387216.2020.1716822

9. Yu, J. (2018). The belt and road initiative: domestic interests, bureaucratic politics and the EU-China relations. Asia Europe Journal, 16(3), 223–236, p. 227.

10. Patton, D. (2018, November 12). Central Asia-China gas pipeline to hit maximum capacity—PetroChina. Reuters. Retrieved from https://af.reuters.com/article/energyOilNews/idAFL4N1XN3DF

11. CNPC News. (2019, April 17). Zhongya tianranqi guandao leiji xiang zhongguo rushutianranqi 2632 yibiaofang [Central Asia-China gas pipeline (CACGP) supplied China 2632 billion cubic meters]. CNPC. Retrieved from http://cnenergy.org/yq/trq/201904/t20190417_754710.html

12. Li, M. (2016). From Look-west to act-west: Xinjiang's role in China–central Asian relations. Journal of Contemporary China. 100 (25), 515–528.

13. Wang, J. (2012, October 17). Xijin, zhongguo diyuanzhanlve de zaipingheng [Act west, rebalancing of China's geopolitical strategy]. Global Times. Retrieved from https://opinion.huanqiu.com/opinion_world/2012-10/3193760.html?agt=15422

14. Zhao, H. (2011). Sichou zhilu de guanzhudian he guanqiedian [Concerns and breakthroughs Points of the Silk Road Economic Belt]. Journal of Xinjiang Normal University, 35(3), 27–36.

15. Yan. (2018, June 7). China, Kyrgyzstan agree to establish comprehensive strategic partnership. Xinhua News. Retrieved from http://www.xinhuanet com/english/2018-06/07/c_137235571_2.htm

16. The full name of the declaration is "Joint Declaration on New Stage of Comprehensive Strategic Partnership Between the People's Republic of China and the Republic of Kazakhstan."

17. The National Development and Reform Commission of the People's Republic of China, formerly State Planning Commission and State Development Planning Commission, is a macroeconomic management agency under the Chinese State Council, which has broad administrative and planning control over the Chinese economy.

18. Chen, A. (2018, August 23). China's CNPC upgrade at Kazakh's Shymkent refinery. Reuters. Retrieved from https://af.reuters.com/article/commoditiesNews/idAFL3N1VE1PR

19. Kukeyeva, F., Ormysheva, T.A., Baizakova, K., & Augan, M.A. (2018). Is Ili/Irtysh rivers: A 'casualty' of Kazakhstan-China relations. Academy of Strategic Management Journal. 17, 1–12.

20. Baizakova, Z. (2015). The Irtysh and Ili Transboundary Rivers: The Kazakh-Chinese Path to Compromise. Central Asia Program, George Washington University. Retrieved from: https://centralasiaprogram.org/archives/7374

THE BRI III

21. Hurley, J., Morris, S., Portelance, G. & Portelance, G. (2018). Examining the Debt Implications of the Belt and Road Initiative from a Policy Perspective "Examining the Debt Implications of the Belt and Road Initiative from a Policy Perspective." CGD Policy Paper. Washington, DC: Centre for Global Development. Retrieved from www.cgdev.orgwww.cgdev.org

22. Aminjonov, F., Abylkasymova, A., Aimée, A., Eshchanov, B., Moldokanov, D., Overland, I., & Valkulchuk, R. (2019). BRI in Central Asia: Overview of Chinese Projects. Central Asia Regional Data Review, 20, 1–5.

23. China-Kazakhstan cooperation: Lianyungang Port in Jiangsu Province links up Kazakhstan. (2018, June 04). China Global Television Network. Retrieved from https://news.cgtn.com/news/344d6a4d32454464776c6d636a4e6e62684a4856/share_p.html

24. Fields D., Kochnakyan A., Stuggins G., Jones B. J., Tajikistan's Winter Energy Crisis: electricity supply and demand alternatives. The World Bank. (Report No. 75198). Washington, D.C.: Retrieved from http://documents1.worldbank.org/

25. Idrisova, N., & Earth, L. (2018, January 17). A second coal fired power plant for the Tajik capital. Bankwatch Network. Retrieved from https://bankwatch.org/blog/a-second-coal-fired-power-plant-for-the-tajik-capital

26. van der Kley, D. (2018, April 14). The Full Story Behind China's Gold Mine-Power Plant Swap in Tajikistan. The Diplomat. Retrieved from https://thediplomat.com/2018/04/the-full-story-behind-chinas-gold-mine-power-plant-swap-in-tajikistan/

27. Zhang, R., & Li, D. (2018, October 13). Chinese companies bring warmth, convenience to Central Asian people. Xinhua News. Retrieved from http://www.xinhuanet.com/english/2018-10/13/c137530521.htm

28. Helping Tajikistan build power "lifeline." (2015, April 20). TBEA Co. Retrieved from https://www.tbea.com/cs/Satellite?c=Page&cid=1467897312566&d=Touch&pagename=TBEA_EN%2FPage%2FENTemplate%2FNewsCenter%2FNewsInfo&num=15&assetid=1467897318145

29. Idrisova, N., & Earth

30. Mogilevsky, R. (2019). Kyrgyzstan and the Belt and Road Initiative. (Working paper 50). Bishkek: Retrieved from https://www.ucentral-asia.org/Content/downloads/UCA-IPPA-Wp50%20-%20ENG.pdf

31. Ibid.

32. Ibid.

33. Lain, S. (2016, April 27). China's Silk Road in Central Asia: transformative or exploitative? Financial Times. Retrieved from https://www.ft.com/content/55ca031d-3fe3-3555-a878-3bcfa9fd6a98

34. van der Kley, D. (2020). Chinese Companies' Localization in Kyrgyzstan and Tajikistan. *Problems of Post-Communism*, 1–10.

35. Mogilevsky, Kyrgyzstan and the Belt and Road Initiative, p. 14.

36. Belt and Road News, China's BRI extends to Kyrgyzsyan, but are new transport links worth all that debt? (2019, April 28). Retrieved from https://www.beltandroad.news/2019/04/28/chinas-bri-extends-to-kyrgyzstan-but-are-new-transport-links-worth-all-that-debt/

37. Ibid, p.7.

38. Kyrgyzstan asks China for grant instead of loan. Eurasianet. (2019, February 28). Eurasianet. Retrieved from https://eurasianet.org/kyrgyzstan-asks-china-for-grant-instead-of-loan

39. Mogilevsky, Kyrgyzstan and the Belt and Road Initiative.

40. Osh-Batken-Isfana Road Rehabilitation Project, Ministry of Transport and Roads of the Kyrgyz Republic, Retrieved June 6, 2020 from http://piumotc.kg/en/osh-batken-isfana/

41. Osh-Istafa project document. (2010). The World Bank (Report No. AB3510) Retrieved from http://documents1.worldbank.org/curated/en/128611468047374247/pdf/PID0Osh0Isfana0Road010Concept0Stage0v3.pdf

42. In the Kyrgyz Republic: A new road ties trade and towns together. (2013). The World Bank. Retrieved from https://www.worldbank.org/en/results/2013/06/20/kyrgyz-republic-new-road-ties-trade-and-townstogether

43. Burkhanov, A. (2018). The Impact of Chinese Silk Road Strategy on National Identity Issues in Central Asia: A Media Review. In Laruelle, M. (Ed). China's belt and road initiative and its impact in central Asia. George Washington University, Central Asia Program.

44. Garibov, A. (2018). Contemporary Chinese Labor Migration and Its Public Perception in Kazakhstan and Kyrgyzstan. In Laruelle, M. (Ed). China's belt and road initiative and its impact in central Asia. George Washington University, Central Asia Program, p.147.

45. Peyrouse, S. (2016). Discussing China: Sinophilia and sinophobia in Central Asia, *7*(1), 14–23.

46. Tritto, A., & Camba, A. (2019, April 15). The Belt and Road: The Good, the Bad, and the Mixed. The Diplomat. Retrieved from https://thediplomat.com/2019/04/the-belt-and-road-the-good-the-bad-and-the-mixed/

47. Brautigam, D. (2019). Misdiagnosing the Chinese infrastructure push. The American Interest, 4. Retrieved from https://www.the-american-interest.com/2019/04/04/misdiagnosing-the-chinese-infrastructure-push/

48. Eshaliyeva, K. (2019, March 13). Is anti-Chinese mood growing in Kyrgyzstan? *Open Democracy.* Retrieved from https://www.opendemocracy.net/en/odr/anti-chinese-mood-growing-kyrgyzstan/

49. Lelik, A. (2015, February 10). Kyrgyzstan: Nationalist Vice Squad Stirs Controversy. Eurasianet. Financial Times. Retrieved from https://eurasianet.org/kyrgyzstan-nationalist-vice-squad-stirs-controversy

50. Garibov, Contemporary Chinese Labor Migration.

51. The survey was conducted by Social and Marketing Research Agency 'BRiF Central Asia' (Almaty).

52. The eastern region saw an increase from 12% in 2007 to 36% in 2012, and the central region from 25% in 2007 to 50% in 2012.

53. Sadovskaya, Y. & Utyasheva, L. (2018). "Human Silk Road": The People-to-People Aspect of the Belt and Road Initiative. In Laruelle, M. (Ed). China's Belt and Road Initiative and its impact in Central Asia. George Washington University, Central Asia Program, p. 123.

54. Ibid, p. 124.

55. Sadovskaya & Utyasheva, "Human Silk Road."

56. Following independence, Uzbekistan and Turkmenistan both took gradual approaches to economic reform, whilst Tajikistan's ability to undertake reform was impeded by its civil war that broke out the year after independence. Other factors also restrict trade for these countries, such as Tajikistan's limited infrastructural development, Turkmenistan's command-style economy and Uzbekistan's political relations with neighbouring countries.

57. See e.g. Botoeva, A., & Spector, R. (2013). Sewing to Satisfaction: Craft-based Entrepreneurs in Contemporary Kyrgyzstan. Central Asian Survey 32, 487–500 and Andreoni, A., & Chang, H-J. (2017). Bringing Production and Employment Back into Development. Cambridge Journal of Regions, Economy, and Society, 10(1).

58. Botoeva & Spector, Sewing to Satisfaction.

59. Alff, H. (2015). Profiteers or Moral Entrepreneurs?: Bazaars, Traders and Development Discourses in Almaty, Kazakhstan. International Development Planning Review, 37(3), 249–267.

60. Ibid, p. 254.

61. Alff, H. (2016). Flowing goods, hardening borders? China's commercial expansion into Kyrgyzstan re-examined. *Eurasian Geography and Economics, 57*(3), 433–456.

62. Ibid, p. 444.

63. Alff, Profiteers or Moral Entrepreneurs?, p. 255.

64. Alff, Flowing goods, p. 443.

65. Ibid, p. 444.

66. Ibid.

67. Ibid, p. 450.

68. Ibid.
69. Marsden, M. (2016b). 'We Are Both Diplomats and Traders':
Afghan Transregional Traders across the Former Soviet Union. *Cambridge Anthropology, 34*(2), 59–75, p. 63.
70. Alff, Profiteers or Moral Entrepreneurs?, p. 257.
71. Karrar, H. (2017). Kyrgyzstan's Dordoi and Kara-Suu Bazaars:
Mobility, Globalization and Survival in Two Central Asian Markets. Globalizations, 14(4), 643–657, p. 653.
72. See e.g. Putz, C. (January 10, 2018). Full of gold: Chinese company which sacked Kyrgyz miners claims hard times. *The Diplomat.* Retrieved from   https://thediplomat.com/2018/01/full-of-gold-chinese-company-which-sacked-kyrgyz-miners-claims-hard-times/

CONCLUSION

GLOBAL COOPERATION, PAST AND FUTURE

Central Asia and China are undeniably bound together: for millennia, people, goods and ideas moved across this region unimpeded. When we consider the long history of Eurasia, it becomes clear that the present arrangement of borders in the region is anomalous: the current border between Xinjiang and the Central Asian states cuts through a region that has never before been divided in this way. Especially in light of the deep ethnic, religious and cultural commonalities between China and Central Asia, greater cooperation between the two makes obvious sense.

And indeed, there has been a clear trend in Asia towards cooperation. The BRI draws upon the concept of the Ancient Silk Road in its central aim of increasing connectivity across Eurasia. However, as we have demonstrated in preceding chapters, this trend towards cooperation was already happening prior to the announcement of the BRI in 2013. It was happening at the state level through the establishment of a multilateral institution, the Shanghai Cooperation Organisation (SCO), which both promoted dialogue and brought about concrete action. Participation by China and the Central Asian states in the SCO helped to facilitate Chinese investment in trade, infrastructure and hydrocarbons in Central Asia. The trend towards cooperation was also already happening at the interpersonal level, particularly through itinerant trade, which has enabled Chinese and Central Asian traders to build relationships with one another. This book has shown that the BRI is further strengthening these relationships and cooperative strategies, rather than imposing an entirely new economic regime upon China's neighbours. It is formalising and upgrading China's longstanding diplomacy and investment in Central Asia, and drawing upon pre-existing economic ideas and practice within the China-Central Asia relationship.

Whilst we have seen a trend towards cooperation in Asia, we have simultaneously witnessed the implementation of isolationist policies in the U.S. and Europe, such as Brexit, and the U.S.'s withdrawal under President Trump from the Trans-Pacific Partnership and the Paris agreement. However, the authors of this book do not advocate simply for "more globalisation," since globalisation can take many forms. Openness of trade and the establishment of multilateral institutions are not solutions in and of themselves. Firstly, free trade does not always benefit everyone equally, as shown by the longstanding opposition of Russia and the Central Asian countries to China's proposal of an Asian free trade area. Secondly, some of the world's most influential multilateral institutions, such as the IMF and the WTO, were set up following World War Two on U.S. terms, and at the expense of other nations' interests. From the 1980s onwards these "Bretton Woods" institutions began to aggressively promote the implementation of neoliberal economic policies—such as privatisation and market liberalisation—across the world. This produced a new form of globalisation with reduced state intervention and freely flowing financial capital, leading to massive inequality both globally and within countries, and the concentration of wealth in the hands of a small global elite. The BRI, however, offers an opportunity to try out different, more equitable, international governance mechanisms that might constitute a more "inclusive" globalisation. Liu Weidong argues that a new model of global economic governance "needs to take into account the social interests of ordinary people, to extend modern infrastructure to more areas and to ensure that economic growth benefits more people."[1] The BRI promotes the idea of shared growth through collaboration, connectivity and mutual learning.[2] Whilst the BRI is China-led, BRI projects themselves do not always follow a China-centric approach. As shown in chapter 4, projects in Central Asia involve non-Chinese actors and are designed to align with participant countries' own development models: China has emphasised that each country must choose the development path that is right for its own situation. However, whilst BRI has been inclusive at the national level, its inclusiveness at the subnational level may be restricted, since inevitably the ruling elites within each BRI state make the key decisions about development strategy and may not take steps to address existing inequalities or the marginalisation of different groups within their country. This applies to China as well as the BRI states.

There are many aspects of the BRI which could be viewed as positive developments. Multilateral cooperation and the strengthening of intercultural understanding are both essential for diffusing tensions and preventing conflict. One example of how the BRI is bringing about more inclusive globalisation is its central aim of improving infrastructure. Infrastructure requires long-term funding, and the BRI provides this "patient capital" which the global infrastructure financing market, with its short-termist approach, does not. This is particularly valuable to countries such as those in Central Asia whose governments cannot themselves easily provide this capital. Infrastructure enables economic connections to be made in the region, and has the potential to improve living standards, especially in Central Asia, which has long struggled from poor transportation networks. Furthermore, regional cooperation also enables transnational green projects—which bring collective benefit—to be implemented, such as the recent initiative to plant the Euphrates Poplar across Central Asia.[3]

The BRI is a major opportunity for China to take a lead on reducing greenhouse gas emissions and pioneering transnational green development projects across the Belt and Road countries. Its interactions with these countries should be used to promote mutual support for rapid action to tackle climate change and ecological breakdown. Whilst China has promised to do this, and is taking substantial action on this front, this action is marred by its continuing investments in fossil fuels. Alongside these concerns over carbon emissions, there are many other aspects of the BRI which may prove harmful, such as countries taking on high levels of debt due to Chinese loans. Some of these issues are well within China's power to mitigate. However, even if it does so, it is important to acknowledge that for multiple countries to work together is never straightforward or automatic: the BRI will undoubtedly encounter problems throughout its implementation.

Rather than being a carefully executed masterplan, as is often implied in European and U.S. commentary, the BRI is instead still a work-in-progress with much that remains unclear at the level of domestic decision-making. At present, it more resembles a large umbrella under which diverse projects are placed. We suggest that the BRI does not need to be assessed as "overall" a beneficial or harmful project: in any case, it is too massive and diverse a project for this kind of assessment to be feasible. What is needed is a greater understanding of local contexts in which specific BRI projects are operating. This is what this book has begun to do for Central Asia, albeit briefly. We have given an overview of the history of the region and examined a select number of case studies to show the impact of the BRI on a local level. Part of our aim in doing this has been to highlight the historical and current importance of Central Asia in global economic networks.

At the crossroads of Eurasia, Central Asia has been crucial to the economics of the region for thousands of years. It reached its peak of trade and prosperity with the emergence of the Mongol Empire, whose rulers were indigenous to the region. The Mongols drew upon their nomadic philosophy to inform their methods of governance, such as their tolerance of cultural differences and a multilateral approach that allowed different parts of the empire to cooperate whilst maintaining a substantial degree of independence.

The institutions set up by the Mongols to facilitate trade put Central Asia right at the heart of a huge and uninterrupted network stretching from eastern China to Europe. However, Central Asia's incorporation into the Chinese and Russian Empires five centuries later rendered it less visible. With the decline of the Silk Road, as well as Soviet restrictions on trade, it no longer occupied its central position in the Eurasian trade network. In analyses of Eurasia today, it is still often seen as playing a passive role, underdeveloped and hemmed in between larger powers.

Nonetheless, the geographical position of the region remains a defining feature. Central Asia is a focus of the BRI due to its gateway location within the Eurasian landmass. We have demonstrated that Kyrgyzstan and Kazakhstan are especially important in enabling goods to move across Eurasia. The multiple ethnic, linguistic and religious connections between Central Asians and their neighbours enable the former to make connections, both social and economic, beyond their own country's borders. The mobility of itinerant traders relies on this geography and shared culture. The success of the Mongols, as well as the region's long history throughout which people and goods moved constantly, suggests that the landlocked countries of Central Asia are more suited to cooperation than to nationalist isolation.

Through looking at different forms and levels of cooperation between China and Central Asia, the discussion we have had in this book challenges the common perception in western media that the non-western powers' role in international relations is a zero-sum game. The fear, often implied and sometimes explicitly stated, that the BRI constitutes some kind of Chinese scheme for world domination, is not based on any convincing evidence at present. It seems more likely that a multipolar world will arise, with several major powers in existence: though this would mean the displacement of the U.S. as the sole dominant global power, and of course this is not desirable to those who benefit from U.S. dominance.

Fears of China are also fed by widespread misperceptions and a lack of in-depth understanding of it. Central Asia, as well as other non-Western states, are likewise subject to misperceptions, though being smaller powers, the Central Asian states do not inspire fear. These misperceptions must be addressed: apart from anything else, they are likely to result in the adoption of misguided and potentially harmful diplomatic strategy towards these countries. An active effort is required on the part of other nations and powers to deepen cultural exchange and political cooperation with China and Central Asia.

We are of the view that the strengthening of multilateral approaches and institutions is a positive development, so long as these institutions are shaped by a diversity of nations, with equal voice given to those less powerful ones. What is important is that the rules are not made by one country alone. Echoing Andrew Gamble's argument from his book "Open Left,"[4] we suggest that the best way to strengthen multilateralism is to move beyond a western-centric international order and allow rule-making processes to be influenced by non-Western states.

Whilst the BRI is by no means a perfect example to follow, there is much that the rest of the world can learn from Asia's approach towards international relations and multilateralism. More than ever, many of the problems that countries face are now global and cannot be solved by a single nation. The emergence of the Covid-19 pandemic has highlighted the failings of isolationist policies: public health experts are in agreement that a lack of collaboration has weakened the global effort to limit the damage done by the virus.[5] The sharing of medical resources and coordination of strategies are vital to an effective and quick response, but unfortunately this has not happened across the board. In particular, the US leadership that would once have been expected was absent under President Trump. Whilst China's initially slow response to the virus has attracted criticism, it subsequently delivered huge amounts of medical expertise and supplies to numerous countries, including Central Asia. In March 2020, Xi Jinping told the Italian prime minister that he planned to establish a "health silk road." Of course, this in itself has attracted similar criticisms from commentators as those which have been levelled at the BRI in general: China is trying to gain influence and soft power, and this is suspicious. The headline of an article by Bruno Maçaes sums up these criticisms: "China wants to use the coronavirus to take over the world."[6] These commentators are not exactly wrong: it is inevitable that China's assistance during a time of crisis will increase its soft power, since this is necessarily the case for any country that positions itself as a global benefactor. However, in making cooperation its priority, China is acting not only in the best interests of itself, but of all.

On top of the current public health crisis, all of our other most pressing issues are also global ones, and are interconnected: most obviously, the climate crisis and environmental breakdown, but also migration, food security and many more. There is an urgent need for states to prioritise their obligations to the global community as well as looking after national interests. Asia is still in the early stages of establishing mechanisms for cooperation across the continent, and many obstacles and questions remain. Nonetheless, China and its neighbours in Central Asia have understood that in order to build a better world, countries must work together.

Whilst the realities of the BRI on the ground may be mixed, we suggest that the "Silk Road" has substantive use as a concept that can shape and prompt future action. The representation of space and spatial relationships produced by the Silk Road offers, as the academic Tamara Chin puts it, "a condition or strategy for geopolitical thought and action."[7] The Silk Road speaks of a geopolitical approach that is enduringly cooperative, of an ethical stance that values difference and of an economic system that depends upon relationships of trust across the boundaries of space, language and ethnicity. It provides us with a vision of how differences can coexist alongside each other; a vision that is much needed at present.

NOTES

1. Liu, W., Dunford, M., & Gao, B. (2018). A discursive construction of the Belt and Road Initiative: From neo-liberal to inclusive globalization. Journal of Geographical Sciences, 28(9), 1–17, p. 10.

2. Fang, C., & Nolan, P. (Ed). (2019). *Handbook of the Belt and Road.* New York: Routledge, pp. 3–4.

3. Wang, Y. (2019, Jan). Greening the desert. China report, vol no.68.

4. Gamble, A. (2018). *Open Left: The Future of Progressive Politics.* Rowman & Littlefield International: London.

5. Safi, M. (2020, May 1). 10 key lessons for the future to be learned from fighting Covid-19. The Guardian. Retrieved from https://www.theguardian.com/world/2020/may/01/10-key-lessons-for-future-learned-fighting-covid-19-coronavirus-society

6. Maçaes, B. (2020, April 3). China wants to use the coronavirus to take over the world. National Review. Retrieved from https://www.nationalreview.com/2020/04coronavirus-pandemic-china-seeks-increase-geopolitical-power/

7. Chin, T. (2013). The invention of the Silk Road, 1877. *Critical Inquiry, 40*(1), 194–219.

www.ingramcontent.com/pod-product-compliance
Lightning Source LLC
Chambersburg PA
CBHW050535270326
41926CB00015B/3233